I0541929

PLOT
OR
PARANOIA

CITI OF BOOKS

CITIOFBOOKS, INC.
3736 Eubank NE Suite A1
Albuquerque, NM 87111-3579
www.citiofbooks.com
Hotline: 1 (877) 389-2759
Fax: 1 (505) 930-7244

Ordering Information:

Quantity sales. Special discounts are available on quantity purchases by corporations, associations, and others. For details, contact the publisher at the address above.

Printed in the United States of America.

ISBN-13:   Paperback   979-8-89391-144-2
              eBook   979-8-89391-145-9

Library of Congress Control Number: 2024910583

TABLE OF CONTENTS

INTRODUCTION

The purpose of this book is to introduce the reader to facts not readily available, and in many instances purposefully hidden, about the birth of this country, the framers of the Constitution, and their hidden agenda. This book gives some insights into the problems that the founders of this country faced in convincing the people that they would have a large voice in their government, and freedoms not enjoyed by other countries. And at the same time keeping total control of all monetary assets, making sure that the ruling elites' pockets were lined in a fashion befitting monarchs. In other words, the founders' problem was, how do we keep the dummies under control and working for our benefit without them even realizing that they are still basically slaves? This book plainly verifies the ulterior motives of a sect of founders of this country, by putting forth a wide variety of documentation, gathered from many sources not publicized, and in many instances secret. This book documents the fact that this country was founded by, and is run by, members of a secret religious sect with the ultimate goal of world domination. The key to these accusations is documentation. Herein you will read about signs and symbols encountered daily, such as the symbols on your dollar bill and the Presidents seal, etc. You will learn about what these symbols mean and what they were derived from. Why a pyramid and all Seeing Eye? Why a Star of David? They are all documented by their source. You will learn about the mindset of many of this country's founders. You will learn that there was a faction of honest co-founders who were totally opposed to most of the ideas that the majority of founders initiated. You will be introduced to the secret society of FREEMASONS, and shown in detail, documents outlining their agenda for this country and the world. This book sheds light on Masonic ideology. Propaganda, the tool of the ruling elite, is discussed and shown for what it really is. This book illustrates that the majority of this country's forefathers had their own interests in mind, and not the interests of the people, as they so loudly proclaimed. You will learn that the concept of a new world order is not so new at all. I convey an understanding of why people in general, allow themselves to be blindly lead, and in the process, abused.

Part of my reason for writing this book is the loud cry I have heard lately by folks for a return to constitutional law. I hear the Constitution praised and revered. I decided to study the document to find out why it is held in such great esteem. I had never read it in its entirety, so I decided to make a study of it. What I found out about it astonished me. My amazement did not come about because of its supposed fair and enlightening qualities, but because of its purposeful deceit and contradictive qualities. My astonishment upon reading this document prompted me to further study the Constitution's background and the men who conceived it. This book surely makes strong statements, and is totally contrary to everything we have been taught about our country. I take no pleasure in disclosing my findings to you. My only intent is to tell it like it is. One point I wish to make clear in this introduction is the fact that this book is not, or never was meant to be a handbook geared towards anarchy. This book was not written as a justification for any type of revolt. The book merely illustrates the fact that things are not the way they appear and that we, as Americans, have some serious problems to be dealt with before all is truly lost. I have stated what the problem is and have recommended a couple of solid solutions to assist on the road to freedom. As a law abiding, tax paying citizen, I felt it my duty to author this book. I too felt helpless in the face of such a formidable monster, and decided I owed it to myself and my family, to attempt to rectify the problem the best way I knew how to, despite the monster's ferocity. As one small citizen, I offer my attempt.

POST SCRIPT: Since this book was written, another electoral vote put George Bush Jr. in the White House, even though Al Gore won the popular vote.

CHAPTER I

PLOT OR PARANOIA

It makes no difference where you come from, what race or gender you are... when you examine your first pay check and realize that up to 32 percent has been withheld, you get a feeling in the pit of your stomach that something is very seriously wrong. For most folks this is the first taste of adult reality. From that day forward our conscious and subconscious mind becomes aware of all the serious inequities that pervade our lives. You'll see political promises never kept by either party. You will become painfully aware that no matter what the economy does, the rich folks still have the same amount of fancy cars, summer homes, and 80-foot yachts. You'll see some folks who never hold a job in their lives get by okay on state and federal subsidies. Just a few years ago you may have received a draft notice in the mail, demanding that you go fight a war that made no rational sense. You hear politicians preach change, but nothing ever changes except that your standard of living drops. If you question the order of things you are often told, "well, nothing is perfect," or "well, you can't fight city hall." A little more examination clearly reveals that every aspect of your life is dictated to you. If your dream is to own your home, there is a reality check of county, school and city taxes. Oh, and don't let me forget to mention the 8 to 10 percent sales tax off the top of your net pay. Yeah, that's 8 to 10 percent off the top of your buying power. If you have the feeling that someone is out to get you, "they" say you are paranoid. If you go to the shrink and tell him this, he will do his best to convince you that life is basically plot less.

Some folks, in order to combat these feelings dive head first into nationalistic ideology of flag waving and say, "Yes, nothing's perfect in life, but this here country is as good as they come." Sure, that ideology will counter those feelings of being misused and allow you to carry on with your life, not sweating the details. You might convince yourself that, "what's the use? I can't fight city hall," and far be it from me to attempt to change the evolution of mankind. Then there is the criminal, who sees early on that the deck is stacked and decides that since this is how the game is played, he will be just as crooked as the dealer. There is the crusader, who uses all his energy trying to right the wrongs that he encounters, only to look back and see that all he has been doing is digging a hole in a dry sand dune. Either we nullify our feelings with rationalization, or we throw up our hands in confused resignation, working for our meager wages until we have one foot in the grave.

These are some of the many coping mechanisms people use to combat that hopeless feeling that you have been bled all your life. This is where the story ends for most of us. All our lives we realize something is rotten somewhere, but we can't identify the source of the smell or how to put a stop to it. Throughout history there have been factions of people who pointed the finger at what they thought was the source of the smell. Some were right, some were wrong and some just plain lied. Our history books say it was the forefathers of the United States who, being men of great integrity strove to create a system of true justice for all. And our forefathers pointed the finger at England as being the source of the smell; the Monarch and the despots were the evil oppressors. To this day the prevalent idea is that if we would keep with the basic premise of our forefathers and the Constitution, this country and the world would be a better place for all.

For you folks out there who haven't thrown up your hands in confused resignation or nullified your feelings in a flag waving ideology, the time has come to do your homework... It's time to clean the slate of all patriotic romance. Get your history books out and read them. For once, let us now get the facts straight. The Constitution of the United States of America, have you read it? Let's face it; you probably have not. Take a small poll of people you know and ask them if they have read it. You will see what I mean and understand it. Yet when you enter the U.S. Military you swear to uphold it. You pay taxes to a government that places its foundation upon it. Thousands have died to uphold it. But have they ever really read it? I get sick to my stomach every time I hear someone say, "If we would just stick to the Constitution, everything would be much better for all." Well I have read it, and read it. The first time I tried to read it, I was amazed to find that most of it was so confusing and complex that the average person can't make heads or tails of what our forefathers were trying to say. My first question was, if this document was meant to insure liberty for all, why can't the average high school student understand what is being stated in it? Aside from the fact at the time the Constitution was written, most people could not read. Historians admit that several statements in the Constitution are quite vague. WHY? They could have been specific. A question that was central in my mind was the issue of the Electoral College. What really IS the Electoral College? Why are there so many complicated lines written about it in the Constitution? After reading the Constitution, you immediately wonder what was the forefathers' great concern about the Electoral College? Why is so much space dedicated to it in this supposedly enlightened document? Even though the statements about the Electoral College are complicated, you get the general gist that the Electoral College has to do with WHO chooses the president of the United States.

Some folks would ask, "What's the problem here with the Electoral College? After all, the people choose the president. ' Sorry folks, NO, the people don't choose the president of the United States. Why don't they? Because the Electoral College does the choosing of the president. Well I thought this country stood for power to the people. Why don't the people choose their president? Good question folks. Why don't they? To begin with, who are these so called ELECTORS who choose our president? Who elects them? The people? What are their qualifications??? On this last question, the Constitution is not just vague; it flat out doesn't say anything about their qualifications. Ask what are the names of the Electors in my state? Excellent question. One I can't answer because I've never seen a list posted anywhere stating who they are, not in New York anyway.

If anyone has seen a posted list with the names of the Electors of their state, I'd like to know. Are you saying that we don't know who these Electoral appointees are? That's correct. In an elementary school history book, which contains a copy of the Constitution, I counted approximately 124 lines written about the rules of the Electoral College. Approximately 13 lines were written about the peoples' right to vote. That's right, 124 lines written in the Constitution about the Electoral College, the main tool that can and has nullified the vote of the people. And 13 lines on the peoples' right to vote. These 13 lines consist of who can vote (race), also the age and sex of who can vote. The people who were eligible to vote were, white men 21 or over who owned land.

Women were not allowed to vote at all. Black people were not allowed to vote. Slaves were not allowed to vote. Native Americans could not vote. And people with a previous condition of servitude could not vote. So, if you were a slave previously you could not vote. At first the rule for white men to vote was ownership of at least 300 acres or more of land. But after much arguing the clause of 300 acres of land for a white man to vote was thrown out, changed to white men 21 or over could vote no matter how much land he owned.

Wait just a minute, Mr. Author. What are you saying here? Are you saying our forefathers weren't the kind, just, benevolent men that history, our teachers, and the media make them out to be? "You may infer that, but read the Constitution for yourself." You will see for yourself that the authors of the Constitution were intensely concerned about WHO will choose the president. In Article I, Section I, Paragraph II, right after the Preamble, they start talking about the Electors and continue talking about it throughout the entire Constitution. It is an obvious fact that they were very concerned about who would CHOOSE the president. And guess what? They did not put that job in the hands of the people who would live under his term of office. FACT.

Read On. The next thing they talk about in Article I, Section I, Paragraph 3, is how old the Representatives of the House will be; no younger than 25. The House of Representatives chooses the president if the Electors can't reach a majority... again not the people.

Read on. Article I, Section I, Paragraph 4... TAXES. The next most important issue on the minds of our forefathers was taxes. And of course, this paragraph is extremely vague, leaving lots of room for interpretation by the Supreme Court. Read on to Article I, Section 5, Paragraph 18. This section has always mystified me. Quote, "Each House shall keep a journal of its proceedings, and from time to time publish the same, EXCEPTING such parts as may in their judgment require SECRECY; and the yeas and nays if the members of either House, on any question shall, at the desire of 1/5 of those present, be entered in the journal"

Each House shall keep a journal, and from time to time, (vague). Nothing specific for the people, those people whom our forefathers were so concerned about. Then they go on to say, we'll publish it, except for parts they desire to keep secret. Wait... what's the secret? And they will publish the yeas and nays, IF, at least 1/5 of those present say they should. Wait a minute, folks. Does something sound fishy here? Did they really say that? You can bet your ass they did. After reading the Constitution it becomes evident that our forefathers were very worried about rebellion, revolt, and insurrection. In fact they were intensely anxious about it.

There isn't just one reference to it in the Constitution; there were four. Article I, Section 8, Paragraph 39 and 44. Also Article 14, Section 2, Paragraph 100, and Article 14, Section 3, Paragraph 101 all refer to this thorn in the side of our forefathers. The Constitution strictly forbids any rebellion against it, except for peaceful petition. Let us now devote some thought to this subject. Doesn't it seem odd that the forefathers were so strongly opposed to any form of rebellion, except peaceful crying and whimpering to the governing body? Just a few years before, in 1776, they advocated, justified, and incited violent revolt against the King of England. They even put it in writing in the Declaration of Independence. This fact should sound an alarm in our heads. They are specifically telling us, in no vague generalities, that we will be severely dealt with for acting the same way they did.

Now think back in history and see if anything has been accomplished as far as drastic change in a government, any government, through peaceful whimpering to the governing body. I don't know of any. Let's bring this subject down to easily understandable terms. Picture this... tell the class bully that he should not have done this or that, and ask him to please stop taking my lunch money. Of course, he'd laugh in your face. His course of action would not be deterred one bit because the bully only speaks the language of force. Believe it or not, I do not advocate any form of bloody rebellion. In this day and age it would accomplish nothing. Instead it would make matters worse. Nowadays, because of sophisticated communications and modern weaponry, a bloody revolt is virtually impossible without almost total annihilation of both parties involved. But let it be known that there are other forms of revolt which hit hard, but draw no blood. In fact, I believe they send home a message with swifter force than any form of redress, and they hit harder than any bomb or bullet. But at this point, I won't elaborate any further on this subject. That is reserved for the end of the book.

The framers of the Constitution were very intelligent men; this fact is indisputable. They had deep insight into human character, and generally were multi-disciplined individuals. Many were lawyers. The depth of their insight is evidenced in a passage of the Declaration of Independence that states, "PRUDENCE, INDEED WILL DICTATE THAT GOVERNMENTS LONG ESTABLISHED SHOULD NOT BE CHANGED FOR LIGHT AND TRANSIENT CAUSES; IF ACCORDINGLY ALL EXPERIENCE HATH SHOWN, THAT MANKIND ARE MORE DISPOSED TO SUFFER, WHILE EVILS ARE SUFFERABLE, THAN TO RIGHT THEMSELVES BY ABOLISHING THE FORMS TO WHICH THEY ARE ACCUSTOMED." These men realized that people will eat a lot of crap before they will rise up and try to stop it. This left a lot of leeway in the framing of the Constitution which is loaded with evils, which the people would endure without a fight. The framers knew about the general apathy of the working class in their daily struggle to survive. This daily grind leaves little time to think about, let alone act against a governing body that steals from and lies to, them. As long as some of the worker class (slave class) needs are fulfilled... as long as they are allowed to keep some of their money, chances are good that they won't rebel. These attitudes they knew to be fact.

These men were not only very bright and lawyers, but also had the advantage of supreme educations in the finest colleges of the time. Many spoke several languages and were well versed in politics, both contemporary and ancient. At that time approximately 90 percent of the population could not read or write. When I say they were versed in politics, I mean that most of the framers of the Constitution purposely studied all the great politicians, with heavy emphasis placed on the study of ancient Roman politics. Roman politics was given great respect by these men and studied in detail. Many of the ideas used in setting up our government were borrowed from ancient Rome. These men knew their history and they had a good grasp of sociology. They borrowed the idea of the Roman Republic, and the United States is supposed to be a republic.

My point here is to emphasize the fact that the framers of the Constitution knew Greek and Roman politics intimately. It was important to them because Rome had existed and ruled successfully for a long, long time. (2700 years) There was a mass of information on ancient Rome that had survived and could be studied, and study it they did. Most of them could quote it. The terms electors and senate' were taken from ancient Rome. Our forefathers were well aware of the remarkable exploits of one particular Roman ruler (emperor). His name was Octavius Augustus Caesar. This man was able to change Rome from a republican form of government to a dictatorship run by the emperor, without any fuss from the common voting public. In fact, the people were so sold on Augustus Caesar that they begged him to take all their power. Yet, for all outward appearances, he maintained the guise of a republican form of government. This accomplishment and Augustus Caesar's method of attaining it was deeply impressed in the minds of the forefathers of the United States of America.

How was he able to capture all the peoples' power and still make them think they had a republic? His tactics were used as a guideline by the framers of the Constitution to accomplish their goals. That is to maintain ruling elite, who calls all the shots, while keeping up the front of 'power to the people.' I won't go into a whole history of ancient Rome here, but I will draw a few parallels between Caesar and the frames of our Constitution. The first thing Caesar worked on was his public image of benevolence. He totally convinced the Roman public that he had their best interests in mind, and they bought it, hook, line, and sinker. Secondly, and this should sound familiar, he drew up a new Constitution. He embarked on a campaign of unprecedented nationalism, unification and the reconstruction of Rome. He had the people so convinced of his benevolence that they literally worshiped him.

Hitler was also quite successful with the Augustan tactic. My parallel here is drawn not only with Hitler, but also with the total admiration given by the people to the national hero, George Washington. The people were so sold on him that I would venture to say he could easily have been crowned emperor of the United States, if he had so desired. Anyway, Caesar knew he had to give something in order to receive. He showed his stuff by rebuilding Rome. He built roads, public buildings, and restored 82 Roman temples. The people saw the results and begged him to take more power. The eventual outcome of all that Augustus Caesar did to change Rome was to create a succession of dictators by gradually conning the people into giving up their power to rule themselves. This succession of emperors finally caused the downfall of Rome. The Roman people started out with a government where the citizens had a say in their rule, and ended up with an emperor who finalized the downfall of Rome, all because the people put their total trust in the hands of the ruling elite. Augustus Caesar was very slick and so were our forefathers.

This quote from AMERICAN HISTORY REVIEW TEXT, written by IRVING GORDON in 1968, sort of sums up how the publics' collective mind operates in matters of political leadership. "PUBLIC APATHY. Although the average citizen has little contact with, or knowledge of political parties, he is usually content to permit them to control his government. The average citizen generally restricts his political activities to reading the newspaper and to vote in general elections. The man in the street remains indifferent, even for long periods, to rule by party machine. Only when the machine rules become flagrant and a fighting reform leader appears, does the average man become aroused." Our forefathers were well aware of these social facts. They always knew that the common man, with his nose to the grindstone, had little time for politics and still they make every effort to keep it that way.

Let's get back to another question that the Constitution raises. SLAVERY, on this subject the Constitution was clear, except for the use of the word 'slave'... Slaves were referred to in the Constitution as SUCH PERSONS. Article I, Section 8, Paragraph 43. "THE MIGRATION OR IMPORTATION OF SUCH PERSONS AS ANY OF THE STATES NOW EXISTING SHALL NOT BE PROHIBITED BY CONGRESS PRIOR TO THE YEAR ONE THOUSAND, EIGHT HUNDRED AND EIGHT, BUT A TAX OR DUTY MAY BE IMPOSED ON SUCH IMPORTATION, NOT EXCEEDING TEN DOLLARS FOR EACH PERSON."

Obviously the forefathers knew slavery was evil and immoral. But by the above statement gave the Constitution the power to someday possibly put a stop to it, but not before 1808. In other words they were saying, yes it is evil, but let's keep slavery around for at least 20 years more. After all we can collect at least 10 bucks a head for the importation of slaves, not to mention their usefulness. Oh yes, just to keep the record straight, the Constitution has another clause about slavery.

Article IV, Section 2, Paragraph 76. "NO PERSON HELD TO SERVICE OR LABOR IN ONE STATE, UNDER THE LAWS THEREOF, ESCAPING INTO ANOTHER, SHALL, IN CONSEQUENCE OF ANY LAW OR REGULATION THEREIN, BE DISCHARGED FROM SERVICE OR LABOR, BUT SHALL BE DELIVERED UPON CLAIM OF THE PARTY TO WHOM SUCH SERVICE OR LABOR MAY BE DUE." Yes the fate of the slaves was signed, sealed and delivered by our great Constitution for at least another 20 years, by our forefathers who supposedly cared so much about human dignity and justice. Forefathers such as George Washington and Thomas Jefferson were noted for being appalled by slavery. But, let's not forget, these men owned slaves. Most of the men who framed the Constitution owned slaves. They were appalled by it, but not enough to free their own slaves. Do we note a little contradiction here?

On with the Constitution. Here is another real mind bender. Article I, Section 9, Paragraph 50. "NO TITLE OF NOBILITY SHALL BE GRANTED BY THE U.S. AND NO PERSON HOLDING ANY OFFICE OF PROFIT OR TRUST, UNDER THEM, SHALL, WITHOUT THE CONSENT OF CONGRESS, ACCEPT OF ANY PRESENT, EMOLUMENT OFFICE OR TITLE, OF ANY KIND WHATEVER, FROM KING, OR PRINCE OR FOREIGN STATE." Wow, what a mouthful! Even the historians had trouble with this one. Here is a quote from a history book printed in 1952, written by RALPH VOLNEY HARLOW, about this paragraph of the Constitution, "THE SECOND PART IS NOT ENTIRELY CLEAR. DOES CONGRESS HAVE TO PASS A SPECIAL LAW TO PERMIT AN AMERICAN OFFICIAL TO ACCEPT ANY GIFT OR DECORATION FROM ANY FOREIGN GOVERNMENT." Now mind you, the common people were supposed to understand all this stuff, live by it and die for it. Remember, our presidents, military police, paramilitary, etc., all must swear to uphold all of this and be ready to die for it. At this point, if I haven't raised some suspicion, there is really no reason to read on any further. Just go outside, raise your flag up, then go watch the game on the tube.

THE BILL OF RIGHTS... was never meant to be part of the Constitution. It was thrown in at the last minute as a compromise for the Anti-federalists. In fact, the Anti-federalists were totally against the Constitution as it is written. In essence, they thought it was a piece of garbage drafted by rich guys. You see, it was the Federalists who came up with brainstorm for our existing Constitution. The Federalists were in fact a group of wealthy landowners and businessmen who included in their ranks George Washington, James Madison, John Jay, Thomas Jefferson, Ben Franklin, Alexander Hamilton, and a whole lot more. In fact the convention to draw up a Constitution was held in secret, to be attended by a select few. I quote now from the fore mentioned author, R. V. Harlow. "Having done all they could in convention to assure success for their work, the members sent the new frame of government to the old Congress, then setting in New York. Congress, in turn, sent copies to the different States. Because the convention (the convention to draw up our Constitution) had operated under a rule of strict secrecy, there had been no public discussions of this great project, and nobody but the members had any knowledge of what the Constitution was like."

Is it any wonder that once the secret was out of the bag that large portions of the population, in fact the majority, of common folks were outraged by our Constitution. Oh yeah, maybe you weren't aware of the fact that not everybody was buying this Constitution at the time of its inception. Up till this moment you may not have been aware that the framers tried to get this Constitution passed without the peoples' knowledge. Once it was exposed, most folks didn't want any part of it. This historical fact was played down to such an extent, that this knowledge is almost non-existent in our modern day. But a search of old history books and documents will reveal it.

If you think I am blowing hot air about the fact that the people did not want this Constitution, here is a direct quote from one of our few non-Masonic forefathers named... PATRICK HENRY, he told his followers, and he had many, that he looked upon "THAT PAPER AS THE MOST FATAL PLAN THAT COULD POSSIBLY BE CONCEIVED TO ENSLAVE A FREE PEOPLE" (This is another quote from R. V. Harlow's history book.) Also, let's remember that at the first drafting of the Constitution there was no Bill of Rights included. As I said, the Bill of Rights was a bone thrown to the people because of their outrage at the Constitution. Also understand that I personally am not unique in finding the wording of the Constitution confusing. Another quote from R. V. Harlow's history book, 1952; OTHER LEADERS IN THE ANTI-FEDERALIST GROUP (WHO REPRESENTED COMMON NON ARISTOCRATIC PEOPLE) COMPLAINED OF LACK OF CLEARNESS IN THE WORDING OF THE CONSTITUTION: THEY THOUGHT (WITH GOOD CAUSE) THAT THEY FOUND PROOF OF AN INTENTION TO DECEIVE THE COMMON PEOPLE." I didn't find out about these historical quotes until after I read the constitution and my suspicion were aroused. Then, come to find out, there was a whole faction of people at the time, in fact most common people, who thought the same thing about the Constitution as I did after reading it.

CHAPTER II

THE MASONS

You may have noticed in reading this book that the word secret is mentioned several times in reference to historical facts put forth so far. Secret, secret, why all the secrets? Well, the answer to some of the forefathers' reasons for secrets should be quite obvious now, after hearing some historical facts. Obviously the forefathers had some things to hide. One secret that is not put forth in your average history textbook is the fact that most of the men who drafted the Constitution were not only the most influential men of their time, but they were members of a secret organization... the same as today. That's the way the use of secrecy came so easily to our forefathers. The name of the worldwide secret society they belonged to was the FREE AND ACCEPTED MASONS. Yes, a secret society with coded language, secret signs, symbols, and a secret agenda, the NEW WORLD ORDER. * see plate # 1

The term, NEW WORLD ORDER, didn't really become a public term, until President George Bush used it openly in some of his speeches. But the term has been around in Masonic circles for many, many years. In fact it has been right under our noses since it was placed on the back of our one dollar bill, under the pyramid and the all seeing eye. In Latin, NOV US ORDO SECLORUM, a new world order. The pyramid and the all Seeing Eye is a famous MASONIC SYMBOL within the circle of the Masonic Brotherhood. There is another Masonic Symbol on the one-dollar bill that most folks would find strange. Above the eagle on the back of the bill,

* (see plates 1 and 2) there is a configuration of stars that form a Star of David. The Star of David you say, that's a Jewish symbol. The Star of David symbolizes the Jewish KABALA. The KABALA, also spelled CABALA, is a Jewish religious text crammed full of magical formulas, secret letter codes, numerology, curses, etc. The magical word, ABRACADABRA, comes from the KABALA. The Masons incorporate the use of the KABALA in their Masonic ritual.

I now quote from two of the greatest and most esteemed Masons of all times. A. E. WAITE and ALBERT PIKE. On the subject of the KABALA, Waite wrote, "NO PERSON WHO IS ACQUAINTED WITH "MORALS AND DOGMA" CAN FAIL TO TRACE THE HAND OF THE OCCULTIST THEREIN AND IT IS TO BE ESPECIALLY OBSERVED THAT, PASSING FROM GRADE TO GRADE IN THE DIRECTION OF THE HIGHEST, THIS INSTITUTION (FREE MASONRY) BECOMES MORE AND MORE KABBALISTIC." That is what the highly esteemed A. E. Waite wrote about the Masonic book, MORALS AND DOGMA, written by Albert Pike (published by author in 1871). Pike's book is required reading for any Mason who strives to achieve high rank or grade in Free Masonry. Here is a quote from Pike's book, "THE TRUTHS SPREAD BY MASONRY ARE BASED ON JEWISH MYSTICAL LORE KNOWN AS KABBALISTIC GNOSTICISM."

Masonic induction ceremonies are carried out within other federal buildings, along with the 200th anniversary of the laying of the original cornerstone of our Capitol Building. This ritual, conducted to commemorate the laying of the Capitol Building cornerstone, by George Washington, was in every sense of the word, a pagan ritual complete with corn, oil, and wine; conducted on federal grounds with federal permission, by the secret religious cult.

I will describe a photo of an oil painting that was part of the article from the Empire State Mason Magazine. It is a painting offered for sale. It depicts George Washington laying the original cornerstone of the Capitol Building. I have never visited the Capitol Building or seen the real cornerstone, so I can't say whether the stone is above ground or below ground. I assume the stone is below ground, judging from the painting of Washington lowering it. The stone being placed underground in the foundation would also be in proper accordance with Masonic symbolism, the Masons being the unseen rulers. Masons often refer to their organization as the underground stream. The main issue here is not whether the stone is above or below ground, but that this cornerstone actually exists, in place in our Capitol Building. The fact that this Masonic cornerstone is actually part of our Capitol Building could easily be verified by official government historians.

By the way, is anyone aware of what the "G" in the middle of the Masonic compass stands for? No, well you're not supposed to know, it's a secret. If you were to ask a Mason, first he would pretend he didn't hear your question. If cornered, he would probably say the "G" stands for God. But, as with most Masonic symbols there are double meanings, the outward meaning and the hidden secret meaning. The "G" stands for GNOSTICISM. This quote by ADAM WEISHAUPT, taken from page 30 of Fisher's book, "BEHIND THE LODGE DOOR." Weishaupt, creator of the "ILLUMINATI" (Masonic membership required) wrote this advice to his new inductees, "PARTICULARLY RECOMMENDED TO STUDY THE DOCTRINE OF THE ANCIENT GNOSTICS AND MANICHAEANS, WHICH MAY LEAD HIM TO MANY IMPORTANT DISCOVERIES ON REAL MASONRY." In Hebrew the "G" is called Gimel, its numerological value is 3, its signification is the camel. It's associated with the sacred name of God in Hebrew (GHADOL). The "G" stands for a symbol of a symbol, the 3rd God. (Whatever that means). Also GEOMETRY, GNOSTICISM, GIMEL, GHADOL, ETC.

Quote by ALBERT MACKEY taken from THE ENCYCLOPEDIA OF FREE MASONRY. NEW REVISED EDITION, prepared by WM. J. HUGHEN 32' and EDWARD HAWKINS M.A. 30', published by MASONIC HISTORY COMPANY of NEW YORK AND LONDON 1915. "THERE CAN BE NO DOUBT THAT THE LETTER "G" IS A VERY MODERN SYMBOL, NOT BELONGING TO ANY OLD SYSTEM ANTERIOR TO THE ORIGIN OF THE ENGLISH LANGUAGE. IT IS IN FACT A CORRUPTION OF THE OLD HEBREW KABBALISTIC SYMBOL, THE LETTER YOD, IN INITIAL LETTER OF THE WORD,............., OR JEHOVAH,

AND IS CONSTANTLY TO BE MET WITH AMONG HEBREW WRITERS, OR THE ABBREVIATION OR SYMBOL OF THAT MOST HOLY NAME, WHICH, INDEED, WAS NEVER WRITTEN AT LENGTH.

Now, as "G" is in like manner the initial of God, the English equivalent of the Hebrew Jehovah, the letter has been adopted as a symbol intended to supply to modern Lodges, (Masonic Lodges) the place of the Hebrew symbol. First adopted by English ritual makers, it has, without remark, been transferred to the Masonry of the continent, (U.S.A.) and it is to be found as a symbol in all the systems of Germany, France, Spain, Portugal, and every other country where Masonry has been introduced, although in Germany only can it serve, as it does in England, for an intelligent symbol. The letter "G" then, has in Masonry the same force and signification that the letter Yod had among the KABBALISTS. It is only a symbol of the Hebrew letter and as that is a symbol of God, the letter "G" is only a symbol of a symbol.

What s all this got to do with the Constitution anyway? In the first part of this book, I raised a lot of questions about the Constitution, which I intend to fully answer. But first I will elaborate on the subject of the contradictions of the Constitution and its vehemently asserted rhetoric about the separation of church and state. AMENDMENT TO THE CONSTITUTION ARTICLE I, ratified December 15, 1791... CONGRESS SHALL MAKE NO LAW RESPECTING AN ESTABLISHMENT OF RELIGION. This statement was intended to separate government from religion, as are many Supreme Court decisions. This fact is well known. On the surface, this constitutional law is supposed to show that the people won't have some religion forced down their throat by their government. This is what the forefathers wanted its citizens to believe. If this is the case, then what is the religious symbol of Free Masonry doing in the cornerstone of the Capitol Building? And the Star of David on the back of the dollar bill? Wow! These accusations are really far out.

CHAPTER III

THE RELIGION OF FREEMASONRY

Let the religion or cult of Freemasonry speak for itself on this subject. We already know by ALBERT PIKE'S own admission that the Star of David is Jewish and Masons study the Jewish Kabala. Now I will prove that the compass, square and "G" are a religious symbol for the religion of Freemasonry. I quote from J.S.M. WARD, a highly esteemed Masonic writer, his book, "FREEMASONRY": ITS AIMS AND IDEALS (page 71). "I AM AWARE THAT MANY MASONS OBJECT STRONGLY TO THE IDEA THAT FREEMASONRY IS A RELIGION. YET, IF THERE IS ANYTHING IN THE CONTENTION OF THOSE WHO HOLD THAT IN FREEMASONRY WE MAY TRACE MYSTICAL TEACHINGS AS TO THE NATURE OF GOD, CLEARLY MASONRY IS A RELIGION, EVEN IF SOME HESITATE TO CALL IT A RELIGION. IN FACT THE CONTROVERSY IS DUE ENTIRELY TO THE USE OF LOOSE TERMINOLOGY. FREEMASONRY IS NOT A DOGMATIC FAITH, BUT IT TEACHES CERTAIN FUNDAMENTAL RELIGIOUS TRUTHS SUCH AS, WHAT IS THE NATURE OF GOD, AND THAT AFTER DEATH MEN LIVE. THESE ARE DISTINCT TENETS, AND NO AMOUNT OF BEATING AROUND THE BUSH CAN DISGUISE THE FACT. I FURTHER CONTEND THAT THE MAIN OBJECTIVE OF FREEMASONRY IS TO TEACH THE MYSTICAL LIFE AND UNION WITH THE DIVINE."

Pages 184-85 of the same book; "FREEMASONRY TEACHES DEFINITELY THAT THERE IS A GOD, IN THE MAIN, SIMILAR TO THE JEWISH CONCEPTION OF JEHOVAH,

BUT ACCORDING TO THE ROYAL ARCH, (A MASONIC DEGREE) TRIUNE NATURE QUITE UNKNOWN TO THE OLD TESTAMENT, VIZ., CREATIVE, PRESERVATIVE, AND ANNIHILATIVE: IN SHORT, SIMILARTO TRIMURTI OF THE HINDUS, WHO UNITES IN ONE PERSON THE CREATIVE ASPECTS OF BRAHMA, THE PRESERVATIVE ATTRIBUTES OF VISHNU, AND THE DESTRUCTIVE CHARACTER OF SHIVA. I CONSIDER FREEMASONRY IS A SUFFICIENTLY ORGANIZED SCHOOL OF MYSTICISM TO BE ENTITLED TO BE CALLED A RELIGION."

I now quote from ALBERT MACKEY 33' another esteemed Masonic writer. By the way, all the quoting I do in this book by Masonic writers is material that is not supposed to be accessible to the public. These books are not for sale in local bookstores, but they are often required reading for those who expect to attain high degrees in Masonry. These books were printed for Masons only to read, and a Mason has to go to great lengths before these books are lent to him to study.

From his book, THE ENCYCLOPEDIA OF FREEMASONRY: ARTICLE, RELIGION OF FREEMASONRY, "THE RELIGION OF FREEMASONRY IS NOT SECTARIAN. IT ADMITS MEN OF EVERY CREED WITHIN ITS HOSPITABLE BOSOM, REJECTING NONE AND APPROVING NONE FOR HIS PECULIAR FAITH. IT IS NOT JUDAISM, THOUGH THERE IS NOTHING IN IT TO OFFEND A JEW, IT IS NOT CHRISTIAN, BUT THERE IS NOTHING IN IT REPUGNANT TO THE FAITH OF A CHRISTIAN. (Wrong, upon study of Masonic religion, Christians should find it totally repugnant) ITS RELIGION IS THAT GENERAL ONE OF NATURE AND PRIMITIVE REVELATION, HANDED DOWN TO US FROM SOME ANCIENT AND PATRIARCHAL PRIESTHOOD, IN WHICH ALL MEN MAY AGREE AND IN WHICH NO MAN CAN DIFFER."

Am I beginning to make clear my accusations about the insignia of a religious cult carved into the cornerstone of the Capitol Building? And I do mean a real Granite stone physically installed in the corner of the Capitol Building, with compass, square, and G carved into it. A quote from ALBERT PIKE 33' by the way, that 33' (degree) you have noticed by now, is the highest degree a man can reach in Freemasonry. They are the elite of the elite, and only men of important social and Governmental position ever attain that degree. Albert Pike 33' (page 213) in his book, "MORALS AND DOGMA": "EVERY MASONIC LODGE IS A TEMPLE OF RELIGION; AND ITS TEACHINGS ARE INSTRUCTIONS IN RELIGION."

Another quote from J.S.M. WARD on Freemasonry. "ITS AIMS AND IDEALS", pages 186-188. "IN REALITY, FREEMASONRY TEACHES THOSE SPIRITUAL TRUTHS ON WHICH ALL RELIGIONS ARE BASED AND WHICH ARE COMMON TO ALL, AND LEAVE ITS SONS TO ADD SUCH FURTHER EMBELLISHMENTS AS THEY THEMSELVES CONSIDER TRUE AND DESIRABLE. NOW IT IS PLAIN THAT, THAT RELIGION IN WHICH ALL MEN AGREE, AND THAT WHICH IS ACCEPTABLE TO THE JEW, BUDDHIST, MUHAMMADAN, HINDU, AND THE WORSHIPER OF DEITY UNDER EVERY FORM, IS ESSENTIALLY AND NECESSARILY ANTI-CHRISTIAN. IN NONE OF THE RELIGIONS JUST MENTIONED DO ALL MEN AGREE! THEREFORE THE RELIGION OF MASONRY MUST BE A RELIGION ENTIRELY PECULIAR TO ITSELF."

Need I show more? Believe me there is more on the Masonic religion, much more. But the real question still remains. Why are their religious or cult symbols plastered on our federal buildings and our money? This is in violation of the Constitution, but allowed and apparently endorsed by our government leaders. This is one serious contradiction with our government and Constitution that stands out, but there are more. Can you say in good conscience, that our forefathers weren't aware of these symbols." Did they just want some pretty designs for the back of the dollar bill? Obviously that was not the case. The reason these symbols are in places where they clearly don't belong is because the majority of the leaders of our government are party to the deception. The men who began this country and the ones who continue to run it are clearly not who and what they appear to be. The facade that purportedly separates church from state, put forth in the Constitution serves a dual purpose. It creates the illusion that the Constitution has the best interest of the people in mind as far as having someone else's religion crammed down their throat. And it culls out all other formalized religious and moral dictates, except the one, chosen elitist religion of Freemasonry, as evidenced by the cornerstone, dollar bill, and quoted words of the many Masonic religious authorities. In reference to our government leaders who appear to be something they are not. Superficially, they are adamant supporters of separation of church and state, but with an ulterior motive of keeping in power, the Masonic religion. I now introduce Supreme Court Justice, Hugo Black.

Justice Hugo Black was one of many Supreme Court Justices who were adamant supporters of the separation of church and state, as well as a member in Freemasonry, and an avowed member of the Ku Klux Klan. Strong accusation there. Is this possible? Hugo Black's Masonic ties are quite provable. His name is mentioned in the Masonic book, titled, "TEN THOUSAND FAMOUS FREEMASONS" by WM. R. WINSLOW, Board of Publications, Transactions of the Missouri Lodge of Research, St. Louis, 1957 3 volumes. Volume 1, page 275. Justices of the Supreme Court identified as Masons by BROTHER RONALD E. HEATON, The Masonic Service Association Washington, D.C. 1969, page 12. Surely he was a Mason as well as 33 other Supreme Court Judges up to 1984. Although I strongly suspect that there were many more than the 34 verified in the book, "1000 FAMOUS FREEMASONS. Because it is Masonic policy to never make known the identity of all their members. After all, it is good publicity to divulge the membership of a few famous Masons, but it is not prudent to divulge the fact that Masons have occupied a majority of top influential positions throughout the past 300 years.

From the PITTSBURGH POST GAZETTE, PITTSBURGH, PA, I will quote a note of resignation from the KLAN, written by Hugo Black to the KLANS' office of the GRAND REALM OF ALABAMA, addressed to J. W. HAMILTON KLIGRAPP (secretary), dated JULY 9, 1925. "DEAR SIR AND KLANSMAN: BEG TO TENDER YOU HERE WITH MY RESIGNATION AS A MEMBER OF THE KNIGHTS OF THE KU KLUX KLAN EFFECTIVE FROM THIS DATE ON. YOURS I.TS.U.B. (in the sacred unbreakable bond) HUGO L. BLACK." Everybody in Alabama knew him to be a Klansman, it was no secret. But in order to run for Senator of Alabama, he had to renounce his ties to the Klan. Only to renew them again soon after his election to the Senate. Upon accepting his KLAN PASSPORT OF LIFE MEMBERSHIP back, he said, "THIS PASSPORT WHICH YOU HAVE GIVEN ME IS A SYMBOL TO ME OF THE PASSPORT YOU HAVE GIVEN ME BEFORE. I DO NOT FEEL THAT IT WOULD BE OUT OF PLACE TO STATE TO YOU HERE ON THIS OCCASION THAT I KNOW THAT WITHOUT THE SUPPORT OF THE MEMBERS OF THIS ORGANIZATION, I WOULD NOT HAVE BEEN CALLED, EVEN BY MY ENEMIES, "THE JUNIOR SENATOR FROM ALABAMA". I REALIZE THAT I WAS ELECTED BY MEN WHO BELIEVE IN THE PRINCIPLES THAT I HAVE SOUGHT TO ADVOCATE AND WHICH ARE THE PRINCIPLES OF THIS ORGANIZATION." Hugo Black was an avowed Klan member. He was appointed to the Supreme Court by Franklin Roosevelt, (another Mason) in violation of the Constitution. These people have no problem violating their own Constitution when it suits their purpose.

Black was a member of Congress when they enacted a pay raise for Supreme Court Judges, raising their pay to $20,000 per year, exactly $10,000 more per year than the members of Congress were paid. The Constitution states that: "NO SENATOR OR REPRESENTATIVE SHALL, DURING THE TIME FOR WHICH HE WAS ELECTED, BE APPOINTED TO ANY CIVIL OFFICE UNDER THE AUTHORITY OF THE UNITED STATES... EMOLUMENTS (profit arising from office or employment; salary; gain) WHEREOF SHALL HAVE BEEN INCREASED DURING SUCH TIME..."

This is what Justice Black had to say about separation of church and state in his radio address. "THE CONSTITUTIONAL SAFEGUARD (which as proved, he violated at will) TO COMPLETE LIBERTY OR RELIGIOUS BELIEF IS A DECLARATION OF THE GREATEST IMPORTANCE TO THE FUTURE OF AMERICA AS A NATION OF FREE PEOPLE. ANY MOVEMENT, OR ACTION BY A GROUP THAT THREATENS TO BRING ABOUT A RESULT INCONSISTENT WITH THIS UNRESTRICTED INDIVIDUAL

RIGHT, IS A MENACE TO FREEDOM. LET ME REPEAT; ANY PROGRAM, EVEN IF DIRECTED BY GOOD INTENTIONS, WHICH TENDS TO BREED OR REVIVE RELIGIOUS DISCORD OR ANTAGONISM CAN AND MAY SPREAD WITH SUCH RAPIDITY AS TO IMPERIL THIS CONSTITUTIONAL PROTECTION OF ONE OF THE MOST SACRED HUMAN RIGHTS." I could keep on quoting this man's garbage and there is plenty more these guys can eulogize for hours. I guess all the above rhetoric is an exclusion of the Masonic religion. I hope this section of the book begins to answer my proposed question earlier of, "Where are these people coming from?" The picture begins to emerge of an elite group of men whose sole employment is to deceive the populace for personal gain and power. And the truth is exactly as it is presented so far. I agree with Justice Black that integration of church and state is a "menace to freedom." And, I believe most folks in the United States believe that also. From past history it is obvious that total discord is the only product of church and state integration. Discord is really an understatement. Death and oppression is more appropriate. It is an understatement to call all of this a conflict of interest, though it is. Purposeful deceit or plotting is more accurate. This bigot, deceiver served on the bench of the Supreme Court for 34 years. Though the framers of the Constitution were concerned with the appearance of freedom of religion. With no state established religion they screwed up and ended the Constitution with; "DONE IN CONVENTION THE SEVENTEENTH DAY OF SEPTEMBER IN THE YEAR OF OUR LORD ONE THOUSAND SEVEN HUNDRED EIGHTY SEVEN."

The pyramid on the back of your dollar bill is a Masonic symbol representing several things to Masons, two of them being economic unity and order. Hence, the pyramid as far as the Masons are concerned is a very appropriate symbol for the back of your dollar bill. I quote from volume 2 of Scottish Rite Masonry, (page 212) 28th degree, Knights of the Sun, "HIS BODY BEING RELIEVED FROM IGNOMINY, HIS MIND MAY NOW DISCOVER AND FULFILL THE MORAL MEANING OF THE CONE OR PYRAMID: THAT FORM OF MATTER FROM WHICH ALL OTHER FIGURES MAY BE DERIVED, AND WHICH IS AN EMBLEM OF PRODUCTIVE

TRUTH, VARIED ORDER (NEW WORLD) NOVUS ORDO SECLORUM, AND ECONOMIC UNITY. IT REPRESENTS THE TRUE MASON WHO RAISES HIMSELF BY DEGREES UNTIL HE REACHES HEAVEN, TO ADORE THE SACRED AND UNUTTERABLE NAME OF THE GREAT ARCHITECT OF THE UNIVERSE."

From this quote you also see why Freemasonry in degrees, leads Christians away from their religion and replaces it with the religion of Freemasonry. The true Mason raises himself up by degrees until he reaches heaven. The Christians believe that only faith in Jesus Christ can raise a person up to heaven. Above the pyramid and all Seeing Eye on the back of our dollar bill are the Latin words, "ANNUIT CCEPTIS." In English this means, HE APPROVES OF OUR UNDERTAKING. Why is all this written in Latin when we are basically an English speaking people? It's just another outward sign of the Masons' elitist deceptive tactics. They are saying and truly believe that God approves of their plan for a new world order. The Masons believe that they have the divine right to rule and impose their morals and religion on the world. This is what ALBERT PIKE in MORALS AND DOGMA says about their divine right to run the show... and his words speak for what Masons believe. "IT IS THE PROVINCE OF MASONRY TO TEACH ALL TRUTHS, NOT MORAL TRUTH ALONE, BUT POLITICAL AND PHILOSOPHICAL, AND EVEN RELIGIOUS TRUTH. MASONRY IS A UNIVERSAL MORALITY," "THE RELIGIOUS FAITH TAUGHT BY MASONRY IS INDISPENSABLE TO THE ATTAINMENT OF THE GREAT ENDS OF LIFE." "IF RULERS HAVE THE DIVINE RIGHT TO GOVERN, THE TRUE MASONIC INITIATE WILL CHEERFULLY OBEY." They truly believe they are God's chosen people. "ANNUIT CCEPTIS." ALBERT PIKE in his book MORALS and DOGMA, he clearly states that free MASONRY is a "LUCIFERIAN RELIGION". This information is the greatest secret FREE MASONRY PRIVY to 33' degrees MASONS, and not all 33' degrees are made aware this fact, but most are.

CHAPTER IV

THE FOUNDERS PROBLEM
AND THEIR SOLUTION

The main idea of this book is the fact that these Masonic overlords have been in charge of this country from its inception. The founders of this country had a great problem to solve. How do we keep absolute control of the country and yet convince its people that they are free? These men had studied history and political philosophy in great depth. They were well aware that history had proven that despotism, or governments that openly stated to the people, "we are running the show," eventually exploded in their faces, and the people revolted. This has happened throughout history, when the people were openly used by the elitist rich and bled for all they were worth. They had little, if any freedom. This was the philosophy of rule for centuries, total repression of the people through sheer force by the ruling class. Because the old form of open despotism by force caused an unstable government, the eventual outcome was revolt. The forefathers of this country were innovators and realized they desperately needed a change in the method of rule and control over the worker class.

The forefathers had to come up with something new to secure all the riches of the United States and make a stable form of government without getting flack from the little people. Better yet, to convince the little people that they had freedom and rights, and to really make them believe they would share in the riches. A big problem to solve... To break this down into more simple terms, how can we stick it to them without them knowing it? How do we hold the upper hand and the money, yet keep the people from revolting? WOW! What an order. The only government that came close to that order was ancient Rome. So they borrowed from the Roman philosophy. They racked their brains trying to figure out a way. Finally their efforts paid off and they came up with some ideas. First of all, they would promote the illusion that the people had the right to pick their leaders. They alluded to this idea with the right to vote. Then gave them free speech. After all, what is the real harm in letting people say or write what they wanted to? The forefathers knew that unless a person has great backing and organization, he can TALK until he is blue in the face and nothing will ever come of it. They were correct about that. They also knew that people were basically apathetic and don't react to what others say or write, as evidenced in the statement from the Declaration of Independence, "SO LET THE PEOPLE TALK. LET THEM HAVE FREEDOM OF SPEECH. NOTHING WILL EVER COME OF IT, EXCEPT TO PROVE HOW FREE THEY ARE AND HOW NO GOVERNMENT IS OPPRESSING THEM. ANY OF THE NEGATIVE ASPECTS OF FREE SPEECH WILL BE GREATLY OVERCOME BY THE FEELING OF THE PEOPLE THAT THEY ARE FREE." In other words, TALK IS CHEAP. With these ideas of free speech and voting, the forefathers were right on the money. To this day most folks are still illusionary in their thinking that they have a say in their government. Convince us they did, and an excellent job of it too.

It is a fact that the victors write history, and for approximately 200 years, the Masons have been the victors. What we read in our history books has been severely tainted and certain issues of great importance are completely missing. Of course, if the whole truth be known, the people would never have been sold on any of the government practices in the U.S. since its beginning. A quote from NEW AGE MAGAZINE, another periodical published by FREEMASONRY to keep its members informed. The magazine was quoting FRENCH PREMIER ANDRE TARDIEU back in 1946. "FREEMASONRY DOES NOT EXPLAIN EVERYTHING: YET, IF WE LEAVE IT OUT OF ACCOUNT, THE HISTORY OF OUR TIMES IS UNINTELLIGIBLE." The above statement is the total truth. One example is the Revolutionary War. We are lead to believe, through the propaganda of our history books, that the Revolutionary

War was fought because the people were being taken advantage of. Well, the little people, (the working class, tradesmen, farmers, craftsmen) were always taken advantage of, everywhere throughout history. In this country they were taken advantage of by the elite ruling class, from the beginning. There was nothing new or unique about the fact. The Revolutionary War was started by the elite ruling class in the U.S. and fought under the guise that, Mother England was abusing the little man. The working class really had nothing to do with starting the war. The elitists, Masons basically, were angry with the elite Masonic ruling class of England. The American Masons figured that England was demanding too large a share of the spoils robbed from the Indians.

The American Masonic ruling class decided not to share any of the spoils with the English Masons. And the war began. The working class folks were dragged in to do the fighting, headed by American Masonic commanders. So actually, if the truth be known, historians should rename the Revolutionary War. A more accurate name would be THE GREAT MASONIC WAR," American Masons against English Masons. I will quote the Masons' New Age Magazine here to give credence to what I so stated above. "IT WAS THE MASONS WHO BROUGHT ON THE WAR, AND IT WAS MASONIC GENERALS WHO CARRIED IT THROUGH TO A SUCCESSFUL CONCLUSION. IN FACT, THE FAMOUS BOSTON TEA PARTY, WHICH PRECIPITATED THE WAR, WAS ACTUALLY A RECESSED MEETING OF A MASONIC LODGE." Isn't it typical? The big guy gets the little guy to shed his blood for the big guy's causes. How did they dupe the public into buying their form of government, which really isn't anything more than SEMI BENEVOLENT DESPOTISM... under the guise of democracy? Give them a Constitution and a Bill of Rights; propagandize about the great victory we won over the oppressor, (England). Immortalize our generals, instill nationalism, and give the people almost nothing. Put it in writing, make it unintelligible, and raise the flag. There you have it folks, the greatest country in the world.

As stated before, the Constitution, at its inception, was not popular with the majority of Americans. People like Patrick Henry made them, as I have made you, aware of these deceptions by quoting from the Constitution in this book. The majority of the populace at the time of the ratification of the Constitution was aware of the following. It was a document conceived by the rich to secure their riches by keeping in power; those who would best suit their goals. The framers of the Constitution realized they would have problems getting the 13 colonies to ratify it. People who could read realized that lawyers wrote the Constitution, and that there was a lot of legal double talk in it. The framers of the Constitution put a clause in it that would make the ratification easier. I quote from the Constitution, "THE RATIFICATION OF THE CONVENTIONS OF NINE STATES SHALL BE SUFFICIENT FOR THE ESTABLISHMENT OF THIS CONSTITUTION BETWEEN THE STATES SO RATIFYING THE SAME. DONE IN CONVENTION BY THE UNANIMOUS CONSENT OF THE STATES PRESENT (NOT ALL 13 STATES ATTENDED THE CONSTITUTIONAL CONVENTION) THE SEVENTEENTH DAY OF SEPTEMBER IN THE YEAR OF OUR LORD ONE THOUSAND SEVEN HUNDRED AND EIGHTY SEVEN, AND OF THE INDEPENDENCE OF THE UNITED STATES THE TWELFTH. IN WITNESS WHEREOF WE HAVE HERE UNTO SUBSCRIBED OUR NAMES." (Names omitted) By the way, what is meant by the last line of the Constitution "the United States the twelfth?" You got me!

It makes good sense that something as important as the ratification of the Constitution should be unanimously accepted by all 13 colonies, since it had the most profound effect on each colony. Personally I see no reason why a Constitution could not have been written up which was acceptable to all 13 colonies. I was amazed when I read the Constitution and found that its acceptance didn't have to be unanimous. One reason that the framers of the Constitution had to put the above stated clause in was because not all politicians back then, as today, were members of the secret organization that conceived the Constitution.

CHAPTER V

THE FREE MASONIC GOVERNMENT
MASONIC OATHS

Not all politicians were sworn to uphold all Masonic decisions. Some politicians back then, as today, were basically honest men with the best interest of the country and its people in mind. But they were, unfortunately, in the minority as they are today. Here are some of the oaths sworn to by Masons which came before any other sworn oath, for any other reason. This quote from the book, "FREE MASONRY ILLUSTRATED," by JACOB O. DOESBURG, PAST MASTER OF UNITY LODGE # 191, F AND A.M., HOLLAND, MICHIGAN. ROYAL ARCH DEGREE; "FURTHERMORE I DO PROMISE AND SWEAR, THAT I WILL AID AND ASSIST A COMPANION ROYAL ARCH MASON WHEREVER I SHALL SEE HIM ENGAGED IN ANY DIFFICULTY, SO FAR AS TO EXTRICATE HIM FROM SAME, <u>WETHER HE BE RIGHT OR WRONG</u>. FURTHERMORE I DO PROMISE AND SWEAR, THAT A COMPANION ROYAL ARCH MASONS' SECRETS, GIVEN TO ME IN CHARGE AS SUCH, AND I KNOWING HIM TO BE SUCH, SHALL REMAIN AS SECURE AND IN VIABLE IN MY BREAST AS IN HIS OWN, WHEN COMMUNICATED TO ME, <u>MURDER AND TREASON NOT EXCEPTED</u>." Sworn under penalty, "TO HAVE THEIR SKULL STRUCK OFF AND THEIR BRAINS EXPOSED TO THE SCORCHING RAYS OF THE SON." ROYAL ARCH MASONS "SWEAR TO VOTE FOR A COMPANION ROYAL ARCH MASON, before any other person OF EQUAL QUALIFICATIONS." a KNIGHT TEMPLAR IN MASONRY SWEARS, "YOU FURTHER

SWEAR THAT SHOULD YOU EVER KNOW A COMPANION TO VIOLATE ANY ESSENTIAL PART OF THIS OBLIGATION, YOU WILL USE YOUR MOST DECIDED ENDEAVORS, BY THE BLESSING OF GOD, TO BRING SUCH A PERSON TO THE STRICTEST AND MOST CONDIGN PUNISHMENT, AGREEABLE TO THE RULES AND USAGES OF OUR ANCIENT FRATERNITY: AND THIS BY POINTING HIM OUT TO THE WORLD AS AN UNWORTHY AND VICIOUS VAGABOND, BY TRANSFERRING HIS INTEREST, BY DERANGING HIS business, by exposing him to the contempt to the whole fraternity and the world, but more ESPECIALLY TO OUR ILLUSTRIOUS ORDER, DURING HIS WHOLE NATURAL LIFE." The oaths in Masonry are numerous and varied. Each degree has its lengthy oaths, with its form of death penalty for violation thereof. There are 33 degrees and 33 oaths. In one of the degree oaths it states, "WE ARE BOUND TO CAUSE THEIR DEATH, AND TAKE VENGEANCE ON THE TREASON BY THE DESTRUCTION OF THE TRAITORS." Meaning the traitors to Masonry.

The members, all members of the Masonic religion are to take orders from the Supreme Council of the 33rd degree. This next quote is a good example of, and pretty much sums up some of the points I've made so far. This is a quote from a letter written in 1861, from the GRAND LODGE OF YORK RITE MASONS of PENNSYLVANIA to the GRAND LODGE of the YORK RITE of TENNESSEE. "MASONRY IS AS OLD AS GOVERNMENT. IT CONSTITUTES A GOVERNMENT IN ITSELF. MASONRY IS SOVEREIGNTY AND A LAW UNTO ITSELF. IT KNOWS NOTHING BUT THE PRINCIPLES AND TEACHINGS OF ITS FAITH. THE PROUD POSITION (OF MASONRY IS TO) STAND ALOOF FROM THE RISE AND FALL OF EMPIRES, THE DISTURBANCES IN STATES, THE WARS OF CONTENDING NATIONS, AND REBELLIONS AND REVOLUTIONS IN COMMONWEALTHS OR AMONG PEOPLE. THE CLAIMS OF A BROTHER ARE NOT DISSOLVED BY WAR, THE TIE ONCE FORMED, IS ONLY SUNDERED BY DEATH." "BY THE ANCIENT CONSTITUTIONS OF MASONRY, A BROTHER, EVEN WHEN ENGAGED IN REBELLION AGAINST HIS COUNTRY, IS STILL TO BE CONSIDERED AS A

MASON; HIS CHARACTER, AS SUCH, BEING INDEFEASIBLE."

Yes, they knew they would have trouble ratifying the Constitution. They knew it would never be unanimously accepted. The fact that they couldn't convert everyone to Masonic ideology, or convince the populace to accept their elitist document as law, remains a burr in their side, even today. They realize that there is a faction of people in the world who are aware of their undertakings. Yes, small portions of people are aware of their undertakings and don't approve, (ANNUIT CCEPTIS). This next statement is one of the few that I can't prove. But, knowing what you now know, based upon the facts, I will relate to you an observation I made recently of the flag of the president of the United States. This flag and what I observed about it, came to my attention just recently. I believe it indicates resentment, and makes obvious the thorn in the side of the ruling elite. That thorn being the non-unanimous acceptance of the Constitution, and the fact that all folks don't buy their ideas. But, it also indicates that most folks do buy the constitutional package and the Masonic ideology that is behind it. Above "E PLURIBUS UNUM" you see 9 stars, and above the 9 stars you see what appears to be 13 balls of cotton. Beside the eagles head you see 4 stars that are out of order, and appear to have fallen from the line of stars. I believe, and I say "believe," because I have no proof that the 4 stars beside the eagle's head symbolizes the 4 dissenting votes that the framers so apt allowed for when the Constitution was written. Obviously, the designer of this presidential flag could have made an even line of 13 stars to represent the 13 colonies, but chose to have 4 colonies drop off in dissent. The round balls of cotton, I believe, represent 13 spheres of influence, (sphere, meaning something round or 13 colonies. This line of 9 stars represents the vote of the 9 colonies accepting the Constitution fully, and their power over the 13 colonies or spheres of influence. I admit this is speculation on my part, but, knowing the facts so far, I'd venture to say it is an educated assumption. The other Masonic symbols I have discussed, the cornerstone of the Capitol Building, and the back of the dollar bill, was not speculation on my part, but strictly factual.

At this point, you may ask how did all the mystery and intrigue come about? How could it be so widespread and powerful? What is the attraction to suck so many influential people into what appears to be a diabolical conspiracy? And conspiracy is exactly what it is, as evidenced by A. E. WAITE; "IT MUST BE CONFESSED THAT THE WHOLE SCHEME HAS A CERTAIN ASPECT OF CONSPIRACY CONTINUALLY PRESENTING ITSELF AND AS FREQUENTLY ELUDING THE MENTAL GRASP." The attraction to this worldwide religion and political society are many. Put simply, it operates as an 'old boy' network. The high-ups in the Masons are guaranteed control of all worldly assets. When I say high-ups in the organization, I strictly mean the men who have reached the 33rd degree.

No, not all influential men are sworn to uphold these blood oaths. But the ones who are not, are in the minority. "SOME DEEPER ASPECTS OF MASONIC SYMBOLISM" by A. E. WAITE, (appeared in American Masonic Journal) "THE BUILDER," edited by REV. JOSEPH FORT NEWTON IN 1915; subtitle "OPERATIVE MASONRY." "THE PLACING OF LODGES AND OF THE CRAFT AT LARGE UNDER NOTABLE PATRONAGE, AND THE SUBSEQUENT CUSTOM OF ADMITTING PERSONS OF INFLUENCE, OFFERED ANOTHER AND QUITE DISTINCT OPPORTUNITY."

How is it possible for a man to hold public office, swear to uphold the law, when his first allegiance is to Masonry? "RIGHT OR WRONG, MURDER OF TREASON NOT EXCEPTED." Let me now present some proof of who has taken these oaths and show that the GOOD men are in the minority. The next quote should illustrate to a degree why Masonic ideals and principles usually prevail in most instances where important decisions are made. It also illustrates why the Constitution is as corrupt as it is, could have been and was forced upon people who rejected it. This quote is from the Masonic book entitled, "10,000 FAMOUS FREEMASONS," by William R. Denslow. Volume # 1, alphabetically listed names A through D. This volume contains 339 pages. It lists FREEMASONS' names and political titles. The total listings include the names of 219 GOVERNORS, 135 SENATORS, 150 CONGRESSMEN, 26 ADMIRALS AND REAR ADMIRALS, 158 GENERALS OF THE ARMY. AIR FORCE,

AND MARINES. Also, 51 CHIEF JUSTICES OF THE SUPREME COURT, 83 JUSTICES OF THE SUPREME COURT, AS WELL AS SURGEON GENERALS, POSTMASTER GENERALS, U.S. DISTRICT JUDGES, AMBASSADORS, AND SECRETARIES OF STATE. This book is not available to the public. It was printed for Masonic eyes only. I have evidence to present that this list of "10,000 FAMOUS MASONS," is incomplete for specific reasons, to which I intimated before and will prove shortly.

Unfortunately, I do not possess a copy of the book, "10,000 FAMOUS MASONS." All these books written by Masonic authors are extremely difficult to get hold of. People who write on this subject put their lives in position of great risk because the truth they divulge is so inflammatory. Also because it shakes the foundation of an empire so vast, rich, and diabolical. People who write of this subject have mysteriously disappeared, and every governmental institution known to man harassed their families. But, and this is my point, I can only prove by my own research, that there was only 17 Masonic presidents of the U.S. I find it very odd that the Masonic revolution has gone to such great lengths to conquer and run this country and others, and as you have seen there is ample proof of their vast power, but apparently have not seen to it that most or all presidents of the U.S. weren't members of their organization. Only 17 presidents are known to be Masons. Of course, the majority of people under the command of our presidents have been members, this is true. But, I find it odd that we can only attest to knowing about 17 Masonic presidents. Still, 17 Masonic presidents is a substantial figure, but I truly believe there were many more than 17. I very much doubt that I will ever be able to prove conclusively, through Masonic documents that there were more than 17 Masonic presidents. The reason for this is the fact that it is not, as I said before, prudent to show evidence that every aspect of government is run by this secret society.

However, it is prudent to boast of the many famous past members, but only to a point. If the conspiracy, put into print, the evidence that the whole U.S. has been conceived and run by its members, this written evidence could backfire. It can fall into the hands of persons such as myself, as well as several other groups who are aware of the undertakings of Masonry. For instance, it could have disastrous consequences for the Masons, if it were made public that 40 out of 41 presidents were Masons. It would draw too much attention to the society and its workings, possibly spurring on more inquiry into the organization and more public disclosure of its true purpose. I know for a fact that not all Masonic activity is put into print, for fear of the information falling into the wrong hands. And, I know that not all Masons are formally identified as such. A quote from ALBERT PIKE 33', "SECRECY IS INDISPENSABLE TO MASONRY." Masonry has 25 "LANDMARKS" that are "UNREPEALABLE," they can "never be changed." Landmark# 23, "SECRECY OF THE INSTITUTION." It tells its followers that to change the requirement of secrecy, WOULD BE SOCIAL SUICIDE, AND DEATH OF THE ORDER WOULD FOLLOW ITS LEGALIZED EXPOSURE." The Landmark also says that as an open society, "IT WOULD NOT LAST FOR MANY YEARS." Also as proof, I quote from, THE MASONIC NEW AGE MAGAZINE, 1962 editorial. "THAT A MAN IS A MASON IS SOMETHING ONLY ANOTHER MASON CAN KNOW, AND THE SECRET OF THE MASTER MASON CAN BE SIMPLY AND SUBTLY COMMUNICATED AMONGST EAVESDROPPERS WITHOUT THE SLIGHTEST AWARENESS OF NON-MASONS. (IT) IS (PART OF) THE CONTINUING AND ANCIENT CHARM OF AGE-OLD RITUALS AND RITES." "MASONS SET THE BASIC POLICIES OF OUR SOCIETY, YET THE ORDER IS NOT POLITICAL, (oh sure!) AND ITS PURPOSES ARE NOT PUBLIC. IT IS RELIGIOUS."

There are other quotes by Masons I have read that basically state, a portion of Masonic knowledge is passed from ear to ear, and never written down. Consequently, there are some details about Freemasonry that will never come to light. The true total number of past and present Masonic presidents will probably never be provable. I estimate that there were at least 34 presidents, past and present, who belonged to Freemasonry. It may even be as many as 40. My estimates are based on the study of political policy making of all 41 of our presidents, and the men whom they were closest to, after serving as mentors during their lifetimes. For instance, I can't say for sure that FRANKLIN PIERCE was a Mason. But, I do know through the study of history that he was a staunch supporter of ANDREW JACKSON'S policies. And I know for a fact that ANDREW JACKSON was a Mason. I can't say that I found, through research, that JOHN ADAMS, our 2ND President, was a Mason, but I do know that all his friends were. ADAMS was a Federalist and he instituted the Alien and Sedition Act, which forbad people from criticizing government. It actually made it a crime, in spite of the First Amendment... a typical Masonic tactic, as evidenced by Justice Black's escapades. I can't say that BILL CLINTON is a Mason but history states that he was a RHODES SCHOLAR, and that CECIL RHODES, whom this scholarship was named after was. He was a big time Mason in England, who advocated secret societies and their world takeover. This is historical fact. I could quote CECIL RHODES with his diabolic garbage, but I will spare you the details. I can also state that BILL CLINTON attended OXFORD UNIVERSITY, and that many other famous Masons attended that school. I can't find anywhere in the history books that GEORGE BUSH is a Mason. But, I did hear him on television refer to GOD as the GREAT ARCHITECT of the UNIVERSE. As far as I know, only Masons refer to GOD in this manner. I could quote hundreds of Masonic phrases referring to GOD as the GREAT ARCHITECT of the UNIVERSE. When I first heard BUSH say that on TV., it was a dead giveaway as far as I was concerned.

So for Masonic purposes it is not prudent to divulge the names of all its operatives past or present. Certain facts can be deduced from the study of history. I have never read in any history book that HITLER was an avowed creep, but I can deduct from his historical exploits that he surely was a creep. Anyway, my educated guess is that there are at least 34 presidents, past and present, who were and are party to the PLOT. I doubt that the whole truth will ever be known in factual format, as to the true identity of all our Masonic presidents. Seventeen admitted to, 34 to 40 by historical deduction. As far as I am concerned , the provable numbers of Freemasons who occupy high positions in government and large corporations, throughout the world, is staggering. The provable figures I have previously stated, who were heads of the U.S. government alone, is enough to raise serious questioning. As food for thought, I will list a few past U.S. presidents who are conclusively and inconclusively, members of the secret society.

Of course , WASHINGTON, JOHN ADAMS, JEFFERSON, MADISON, MONROE, JACKSON, VAN BURDEN, HARRISON, TYLER, POLK, TAYLOR, FILLMORE, PIERCE, there is strong suspicion that LINCOLN was , ANDREW JOHNSON, GRANT, HAYES, ARTHUR, MCKINLEY, THEODORE ROOSEVELT, TAFT, HARDING, HOOVER, FRANKLIN ROOSEVELT, TRUMAN, (it is thought that EISENHOWER was not a member, I say he was), LYNDON JOHNSON, NIXON, FORD, REAGAN, BUSH, and CLINTON. It is obvious after reading many authors on the subject of Masonic presidents, that they shy away from elaboration on the subject. I realize that my statement, (that there were at least 34) Masonic presidents, is bold. And, that there is no way of positively proving more than 17. And, I know that there probably never will be positive proof, so all that is left is educated deductions, which I have done. The study of past presidential policy making and affiliations is another book in itself.

CHAPTER VI

ANTI-MASONIC PARTY

Most old history textbooks contain a section which speaks about a little known fact. Which is, that back in the 1830's, there was a political party called the ANTI-MASONIC PARTY. There were good, honest people back then, some were politicians, but most were average working folks, who were aware of the workings of Freemasonry in government. People back then were very suspicious about rich men running the show. The memories were fresh in their minds about how despots ran their governments. People came to the U.S. to escape the crushing rule of the elitist rich of Europe. They wanted to escape to a country where they could reap the profits of their work, and not have most of it stolen by the ruling rich. So, they were generally suspicious of the governing body. When word spread that a sizable portion of the ruling body were members of a secret society, suspicion grew. The incident that brought the peoples' suspicions to the political forefront was called the MORGAN AFFAIR.

A NARRATIVE
OF THE FACTS AND CIRCUMSTANCES
relating to the
KIDNAPING AND PRESUMED MURDER
OF
WILLIAM MORGAN
and of the attempt to carry off David C. Miller
and to burn or destroy the printing office
of the latter, for the purpose of preventing the printing and

publishing of a book, entitled

"ILLUSTRATIONS OF MASONRY"

PREPARED

Under the direction of the several committees appointed at meetings of the citizens of the counties of Genesee, Livingston, Ontario, Monroe, and Niagara, in the State of NEW YORK.

WITH AN APPENDIX

Containing most of the depositions and other documents, to substantiate the statements made, and disclosing many particulars of the transactions, not included in the narrative.

BATAVIA:
printed by D.C. Miller
under the direction of the committee.

1827.

THE MORGAN MYSTERY AND MASONIC PERSECUTION-------- 1827 to 1836

Ever since Freemasonry has been in existence, it has excited the curiosity of inquisitive people. Books purporting to supply exposures of its alleged secrets have appeared in many languages to satisfy such curiosity. The various Masonic Grand Lodges have, as a rule, refrained from taking notice of publications of this sort, preferring to let reasonable non-Masons draw their own conclusions as to what credibility to attach to productions of avowed enemies, propagandists, perjurers and romancers. A small number of individual Masons, however, have not always exercised calm discretion. Jealous for the honor of their fraternity, they have been inclined, under provocation, to suppress any and every pretense to exhibit to public gaze the hidden things of their craft. Taking account of natural impulses, it is not difficult to explain how some ordinarily law abiding citizens may, under the stress of outraged feelings, become incensed to the heat of a lynching mood.

It is well to keep these introductory suggestions in mind when reading the facts connected with the Anti-Masonic excitement that, starting in the small village of Batavia, in western New York, traveled through the whole state, into neighboring commonwealths and almost over the whole United States.

In 1826, a man named William Morgan came to the village of Batavia with his family. Soon the news got abroad that he was compiling a book which should expose the secret degree work, passwords, grips, and whatever else was taught and done in the Lodge and other Masonic bodies. David C. Miller, a local printer, was to revise, edit and publish the work. A New York City Mason who had been expelled from the fraternity, after having been admitted to membership in a Commandery of Knights Templar, was to supply the work of degrees of which neither Morgan nor Miller could have any knowledge.

The news caused intense excitement among the Masons of the village which then numbered about 1,400 inhabitants. Word was passed to brethren in nearby towns, more particularly the villages of Canandaigua, Le Roy, Buffalo, Lockport, and Rochester. Soon they formed themselves small groups of Masons bent on preventing the enterprise from being put into execution.

Small town excitement explains much. There were, besides, aggravating circumstances which added fuel to the fire. Morgan, who was to supply the material of the book, in conjunction with an expelled Mason, was a newcomer to the village and generally considered unreliable. Miller, who was to edit the material, had received on the initiatory first degree in Freemasonry and had never been permitted to advance beyond that.

Perhaps we ought, for the sake of greater clearness, say a word more about Morgan. He was a Virginian by birth and a stonemason by trade. At the age of 46 (in 1819), he married the seventeen-year-old daughter of a Methodist clergyman of his native state and set up as a trader in Richmond. Some shady transactions caused his sudden departure for Canada, where he became interested in a brewery, near the present city of Toronto. The brewery was destroyed by fire and he returned to the U.S. He took up his trade of stonemason again, first in Rochester and then in Le Roy. His indolence, unreliability, and vindictiveness became notorious. He moved on and finally settled in Batavia.

In every place, Morgan had left behind small debts. If it were true that he was a heavy drinker, this would not have put him in a class by himself in his day and generation. I am inclined to believe that his personal habits were no worse and surely no better than those of other men of his unstable disposition and station in life. Besides, there appears to be no ground for denying the fact that, probably owing to his southern origin and breeding, he made friends easily, often to the detriment of his none too satisfactory reputation, in that he was able to borrow money more readily than he was able to repay it. Indolent by nature and haunted by debt, he was continually on the lookout for the grand opportunity for acquiring wealth at one bold stroke.

Why, when, and how Morgan came to identify himself with the Masonic fraternity appears to be beyond human power to ascertain. No Lodge has been found that could claim him for its own. It is more than likely that he was "book-made." There were in circulation several exposes of Masonic ritual from which a clever individual might glean enough with which to "get by," during the period of unsettled conditions when two Grand Lodges were contending for sway in the state. A man of Morgan's suavity would have no difficulty to explain defects in his examinations by answering that down "south where I was raised, sir," things were different. He managed to visit Lodges and even to be exalted to the Royal Arch degree in Western Star Chapter at Le Roy.

In Batavia, he visited a Lodge, but was excluded from participation in the formation of a new Chapter. The latter experience nettled him considerably, and he was further disturbed by the evident suspicion the brethren of Batavia entertained regarding his peculiar brand of Masonry. His chafing under this suspicion and finding himself treated as unfit for fraternal intercourse by the local Masons may have had much to do with the pushing of his plan to expose the ritual work of the fraternity.

David C. Miller, publisher and editor of the local Republican Advocate, encouraged the design, if he did not instigate it. He himself knew next to nothing of Freemasonry, but with an eye for business could readily be persuaded that a book such as Morgan purposed to compile would prove a good seller. Here was the chance to clean up troublesome debts and maybe a small fortune besides, As soon as the publication had been decided upon, announcements were made, which raised the tempest in the village.

Some hotheaded individuals were for driving Morgan and Miller out of town, others were determined to seize and destroy all manuscript copy and to scatter whatever typed matter there might be found. Various parcels of manuscript were actually obtained be surreption. Fire was set to the print shop, but put out before any serious damage had been done. Miller shrewdly utilized all this for publicity purpose and hastened to complete the book. Thereupon he was forcibly taken and imprisoned on a trumped up charged. with the result that four Masons were indicted for "riot, assault , and false imprisonment," and then sent to county jail.

Enough manuscript was taken away to make publication of the book impossible, if anything written by Morgan had to be depended upon to supply the text. The fact, however, is that an alleged expose of the ritual of the fraternity, printed in England, formed the substance of the work. The manuscript material was more or less of a "blind" the destruction of which could not cause any serious handicap to the resourceful publishers. The small groups of excited Masons who did not know had set their minds upon extorting from Morgan the manuscripts of the "ILLUSTRATIONS," or else to remove him from the state, by fair means or foul. His numerous petty debts afforded so many opportunities for having him sent to jail. On August 19th he was arrested and imprisoned, but bailed out by Miller two days later. On September 11th, the morning following the firing of Millers print shop, he was taken to Canandaigua on the charge of having stolen a shirt and cravat, but was discharged by the magistrate. He was rearrested immediately after on a claim for $2.68 due to an innkeeper. He admitted the debt and agreed to leave his coat as security, but the offer was refused, and he was sent to jail.

The next day (September 12th) a man named Loton Lawson appeared and asked for Morgan's release. At nine o'clock in the evening, he came to jail with one Foster. The amount of the execution was paid and Morgan set free. He left the jail with Lawson and Foster. Suddenly cries of agony were heard. The keeper's wife ran to the door of the jail and observed Morgan struggling with two men to get away from them and shouting, "Murder!" She saw an unknown person strike with a stick a resounding blow upon the well-curb, and immediately after a carriage appeared. Another woman living in the vicinity of the jail witnessed the same scene and heard the cries. She saw Morgan placed in the carriage by four others.

The persons later directly charged with the abduction of Morgan were Nicholas G. Cheseboro (Master of the Lodge at Canandaigua), Col. Edward Sawyer, Loton Lawson and John Sheldon. Two indictments were found against them: (1) for conspiracy to seize William Morgan and carrying him to foreign parts, and to secrete and confine him there; (2) for carrying the conspiracy into execution.

According to the commonly accepted story, the conspirators drove with their victim, by relays of horses, through the villages and towns of a thickly populated region, a distance of one hundred miles, to Fort Niagara, arriving there September 13th to 14th. Morgan was confined in the magazine of the fort, on the bank of the river, near the ferry house. He was subsequently taken by boat to Canada. Arrangements had been to turn him over to Canadian Masons, but declared that they were not yet ready to receive him. The party rowed back to the American side and Morgan was again placed in the Fort. A small group of Lewiston Masons, upon who now devolved the duty of looking after him, sent a messenger to Rochester to ask those who had brought him there to relieve them of further responsibility in the matter. What happened after this is shrouded in seemingly impenetrable mystery.

If we can accept the story told by Thurlow Weed in his autobiography, the perplexity of the jailers of Morgan was solved by a heinous crime, the responsibility for it being indirectly shared, with those directly concerned, by the Rev. F. H. Cuming, who later found it advisable to withdraw from his rectorship and leave the state. The report is that while the deluded conspirators were struggling with the problem what to do with Morgan, A Knight Templar installation took place at Lewiston, at which the Rev. Mr. Cuming officiated, having come from Rochester for that purpose. At the feast following the ceremony he was reported to have pronounced the following toast: "To the enemies of our Order,—may they find a grave six feet deep, six feet long and six feet due east and west. ' Un-Masonic, un-American, inhumane, as the sentiment was, it seems not to have been challenged, though created "the wildest excitement. ' The story goes that coming from the lips of a clergyman, a guest of honor at a Knight Templar banquet, the mischievous utterance, with the added effects of intoxicants freely indulged in at the time, suggested or encouraged a plot to murder Morgan. Col. William L. Stone, himself a Mason, reports a "confession" made to James A. Shedd by a Knight Templar, six months later, from which we gather the following account: On the 19th day of September, eight Masons, having determined to put Morgan to death, held a consultation as to the mode of procedure. It was decided that three of their number were to be selected to act as executioners. Eight folded slips of paper, three of which were marked, were then placed in a hat. According to the plan agreed upon, each man drew a slip, and, retaining it unopened in his hand, walked away immediately after, not being permitted to examine it until he was entirely out of sight of the others. The five who had drawn blanks were to return to their homes by different routes and never to utter a word about the matter thereafter. The three who had drawn the fatal tickets were to return to the magazine of the fort and "complete the design." Col. Stone, after a careful study of all available evidence, expressed the belief that Morgan was taken in a boat to the middle of the stream, at the black hour of midnight," that heavy weights were attached to his body, and that he was then "plunged into the dark and angry torrent of the Niagara."

Incredible as all this may appear, the accounts given by Thurlow Weed and Colonel Stone are accepted by many as true in substance.

At any rate, many who were in their day supposed to be well informed, though never established absolutely, believed in the murder theory. Grand Secretary James Herring, who was instructed by the Grand Lodge, in 1831, to gather from the public records a statement of facts regarding the abduction of Morgan, and who accumulated a vast amount of information, said in a public Masonic address, on June 7 1837: "The general belief is that he (Morgan) perished by violence"

Assemblyman Gross, who "avowed himself a Mason," said at a meeting of the House, on April 4, 1828, that he believed that Morgan was murdered, and murdered by Masons. On the same occasion, Assemblyman Wardell, who also acknowledged himself a Mason, said that at first he believed that there was "not a Mason in this country so deluded and wicked as to commit so great a crime," but that he had changed his opinion, and now believed that "Morgan had been murdered, and murdered by Freemasons," that the commission of the crime was "without excuse or palliation," but that he could say with equal emphasis, "There are no principles of Freemasonry which require a man to act contrary to the dictates of morality and religion." The Speaker of the House said that it was not certain that Morgan was killed, "though conjectures fasten strongly on the belief that he was."

Governor De Witt Clinton, though he did not at any time give public utterance to his personal conclusions with regard to the fate of Morgan, suggested his anxieties on several occasions. As the chief magistrate of the state and the foremost Mason of his time, he was doubly solicitous to obtain the fullest possible information. Early in September of 1826, a portion of Morgan's manuscript of the "Illusions," surreptitiously obtained, had been offered to the Grand Chapter over which the Governor presided, by a Royal Arch Mason. Clinton, on hearing of this, had declared emphatically that an obnoxious individuals violation of his obligation as a Mason was "no justification or excuse for any violation of the law of the State." He had enjoined upon the messenger to hasten his return to Batavia and restore the manuscript to the person or persons to whom it belonged, adding the apprehension that, the "misguided men" in the Western part of the state might still further comprise themselves. Robert Martin, editor of the ROCHESTER TELEGRAPH, told his associate, Thurlow Weed, in later years that he himself had been the messenger and that "Governor Clinton did urge him to return and prevent further mischief, which he would have gladly done, but it was too late."

Immediately after being officially informed of the ascertained details in connection with the abduction of Morgan, the governor issued a proclamation calling upon the state officers and civil magistrates to pursue all just and proper measures for the apprehension of the offenders, and commanding the cooperation of the people in maintaining the ascendancy of the laws.

A second proclamation was published, on October 26, 1826, in which several rewards were offered, one of $300.00 for the discovery of the offenders, one of $100.00 for the discovery of any and every one of them (to be paid on conviction), and one of $200.00 for authentic information of the place where Morgan was conveyed. The third proclamation, issued by Governor Clinton, on March 19, 1827, read as follows:

WHEREAS, THE MEASURES ADOPTED FOR THE DISCOVERY OF WM. MORGAN, AFTER HIS UNLAWFUL ABDUCTION FROM CANANDAIGUA, IN SEPTEMBER LAST, HAVE NOT BEEN ATTENDED WITH SUCCESS; AND WHEREAS MANY OF THE GOOD CITIZENS OF THIS STATE ARE UNDER THE IMPRESSION, end of quote from this narrative.

When all this became public the common people in the U.S. were outraged. As a result, supposedly thousands of Masons withdrew from the organization, in disgust. I emphasize the word supposedly because often the portion of Freemasonry which is exposed to public view is the opposite of what actually transpires within the secret actions of Freemasonry.

A quote from ADAM WEISHUPT, famous Mason and founder of the illustrious "ILLUMINATI" a branch of Freemasonry. "WE MUST WIN THE COMMON PEOPLE IN EVERY CORNER.

THIS WILL BE OBTAINED CHIEFLY BY MEANS OF THE SCHOOLS, AND BY OPEN HEARTED BEHAVIOUR, SHOW CONDESCENSION, POPULARITY, AND TOLERATION OF THEIR PREJUDICES, WHICH WE, AT LEISURE, SHALL ROOT OUT AND DISPEL." Also, "IF A WRITER PUBLISHES ANYTHING THAT ATTRACTS NOTICE, AND IS IN ITSELF JUST, BUT DOES NOT ACCORD WITH OUR PLAN, WE MUST ENDEAVOR TO WIN HIM OVER---OR DECRY HIM." Another member of the fraternity also stated, "THE MAJOR JOB OF THE MASONIC FRATERNITY IS THE CREATION OF A HEALTHY AND ENLIGHTENED PUBLIC OPINION." "ALL OTHER MASONIC ACTIVITIES ARE INCIDENTAL TO THE REAL PURPOSE OF FREEMASONRY, WHICH IS THE CREATION AND MAINTENANCE OF A PUBLIC OPINION THAT WILL SUSTAIN THE KIND OF WORLD THAT WE ALL WISH TO LIVE IN."

Public image is of supreme importance to Masonry. And, as stated above, they will use any means available to maintain it. Back in the late 1700's and early 1800's, the political workings of Freemasonry were more in the open. It was common knowledge that most of the forefathers of this country were Masons. Through the study of early American history, as previously stated, we found out that the forefathers method of running government was often not popular with the common people. There is always a certain amount of suspicion of the rich and powerful, by the common people. When you add to this suspicion the open fact that these leaders were members of a secret society, this greatly added to the distrust. So at the time of William Morgan's murder, this whole Masonic issue came to a head. The common folk were fed up with elitist secret affairs, and Masonry's public image went down the tubes. The only sensible thing for many Masons to do to save face was to pretend to denounce Masonry and go underground. Supposedly thousands of Masons, at the time of Morgan's murder, quit the organization. And, to show their supposed dislike of Masonry, some contrived an idea to prove to the public that they had denounced Masonry thoroughly. To accomplish this, they decided to publish a book, exposing the secret workings of Freemasonry, the idea being, that if the public knew what went on behind Masonic Lodge doors, there would be no more suspicion, because the public would know their secrets.

So, the publishing of the book, "LIGHT ON MASONRY," really had a twofold purpose, to prove that the thousands of men denouncing Freemasonry were sincere, and to dampen public suspicion of the organization. I have read portions of this book and I can tell you with all certainty, that this book exposes nothing of any importance, and it was never meant to. It was written to make the public think that Freemasonry was being exposed. The book, this day, is still made out to be of great importance. It is kept in libraries under lock and key, but it can be viewed publicly by making a request at the library to view it, like it was some big deal. Here are actual excerpts from the book;

LIGHT ON MASONRY; by ELDER DAVID BERNARD
MOST IMPORTANT DOCUMENTS
SPECULATIVE FREE MASONRY;

The Reports Of The Western Committees
in relation to the
ABDUCTION OF WILLIAM MORGAN,
Proceedings Of Conventions, Orations, Essays, &

INTRODUCTION

In justice to myself, I cannot present this work to the public, without a brief exhibition of the facts that have lead to its publication.

Soon after I commenced the service of Christ, Free Masonry was commended to my attention as an institution from heaven, moral, benevolent, of great antiquity, the twin sister of Christianity, possessing the patronage of the wise, the great, and good, and highly important to the ministers of the Lord Jesus. Wishing to avail myself of every auxiliary in promoting the glory of God and the happiness of my fellow men, I readily received the three first degrees. My disappointment none can know but those who have, in similar circumstances, have been lead in the same path of folly and sin. I silently retired from the institution, and for three years was hardly known as a Mason. I was not, however, without my reflections on the subject. I considered what I had taken as frivolous and wicked; but was unwilling to believe that there existed no substantial good in the order; and this idea was strengthened from the fact that many of my friends of a higher grade in Masonry taught me, that what I had received was not the "magnum bonum" of the institution, but that this was yet to be attained. Not being able to advocate its cause from knowledge I had derived of its principles, and supposing that the obligations I had received were morally binding, I could not say "pro nor con" concerning it, without a violation of my conscience. With these views I embraced an offer to advance into the higher orders of mysticism, and reached forward to attain the desired end. In the reception of the Chaptoral degrees, my embarrassment increased. When I came to the oath of a Royal Arch Mason, which obligates to deliver a companion, "right or wrong," I made a full stop and objected to proceeding. I was then assured in the most positive terms, that all would in the end be explained to my full satisfaction. But no such explanation took place, thought I—Is this free Masonry? Is this the ancient and honorable institution patronized by thousands of the great and good? Upon my suggesting some queries to a Masonic friend, he gravely informed me, that the first seven degrees were founded on the Old Testament, and were but a shadow of good things to come; that if I wished to arrive at "perfection" I must proceed to the sublime and ineffable degrees. These assurances, the awful oaths I had taken, with their penalties, and the vengeance of this most powerful institution, combined to deter me from renouncing it as evil. After much deliberation, hoping to find something in the higher orders to redeem the character of the institution in my estimation, I entered the lodge of perfection and took the ineffable degrees.

About this time I learned that William Morgan was writing Masonry for publication. My informer then was a Baptist minister in high standing, and a Royal Arch Mason. He remarked that Morgan's writing Masonry was the greatest piece of depravity he ever knew; that some measures must be taken to stop it; that he would be one of a number to put him out of the way; that God looked upon the institution with so much complacency, he would never bring the perpetrators to light; that there had already been two meetings on the subject; and that he expected there would be another on that day; and finally attempted to justify his murder from Masonry and the word of God.

This conversation took place in Covington, (where I then lived) five weeks before Morgan was murdered; and I should at this early period have informed him of his danger, had I not understood that he was on his guard and prepared for a defense.

The next week I left home for my health, and was absent for some weeks. I returned on the 16th of September, and soon learned that Morgan was kidnaped and probably murdered! I conversed with the Masons on the subject, and they justified both his abduction and murder! I now read the first production of Elder Stearns on Masonry with peculiar interest. I also examined the Monitor and other Masonic writings, and reflected deeply on the nature and tendency of the institution. I compared the murder of Morgan and the conduct of the fraternity in relation to his abduction and the oaths and principles of the order, and became fully satisfied that to continue longer with the institution was not my duty. I expressed my opposition to its principles and the recent conduct of the fraternity in a free and open manner, which caused much excitement among the brotherhood. A meeting of the lodge in Covington was soon called, the object of which was to concert measures for an agreement among the fraternity, in what they should say in relation to their outrages, and to attend to members who were disaffected with their proceedings. I attended for the purpose of freeing my mind. When the lodge was duly opened and the subject introduced, I arose and in the most decisive manner disapproved the conduct of the fraternity, in their violation of civil and moral law. The meeting was long and "horribly" interesting. The true spirit of the institution was peculiarly manifest, especially towards me. For the introduction of Elder Stearns book, and the honest expression of my sentiments, I was most shamefully abused. The he murder of Morgan was justified, and everything said that was calculated to harrow up the feelings of a patriot or Christian. Elder A***, a Knight Templar, being present, boldly asserted, "that if he should see any man writing Masonry, he should consider it his duty to take measures to stop him, that as cities and churches had their laws, with a right to inflict their penalties, so Masons had their laws, with the right to inflict the penalties to them: and that the lodge was a place to try a Mason that if Morgan had been writing Masonry, and his throat was cut from ear to ear, and his body buried beneath the rough sands of the sea, at low water mark, where the tide ebbs and flows twice in twenty-four hours, he could not complain in not having justice done him!" Amen, Amen, Amen, was the response from all.

At the next meeting of the lodge, by request of the Master, I attended. Here a scene passed which language cannot describe! Several hours were occupied in abusing and making charges against me, the principle of which were, I had spoken against the institution. Many questions were asked and insults offered me. I told them frankly I had spoken against the principles of the order; that the right of opinion, the freedom of speech, and the liberty of the press, were privileges given to me by God; purchased by the blood of my fathers; that I had inhaled them with my first breath, and I would only lose them with my last; that if they could remove my objections to the institution, which I then exhibited, well—if not, they could expel me; but if they proceeded to further abuses, they must suffer the consequences. My objections were not removed; and I requested permission to withdraw. Soon after I left them they expelled and immediately commenced a most wicked persecution of me. The "professed" ministers of Christ, infidels, and drunkards, from Buffalo to Albany, were united to destroy my character! I was admonished by oral and epistolary communications to be on my guard, to carry arms; and so great was my personal danger, that my friends would not suffer me to ride alone from one town to another. In short they opposed my interest, deranged my business, pointed me out as an unworthy an vicious vagabond, and object of contempt," and transferred this character after me; and it seemed that they intended to do it during my natural life! The united efforts of the fraternity to injure me, have, however, proved unavailing. I soon became convinced that the peace of the society, the salvation of my country, the present and eternal happiness of my fellow men, and the glory of God, required the destruction of the institution. To accomplish this, I was confident but one effectual method could be adopted, and this was to make a full disclosure of its secrets, To this end I then exerted myself. After an interchange of minds with some of the patriots of Batavia and Le Roy, a convention of Masons opposed to the institution was called, to meet on the 19th of February. 1827. The convention was composed of about forty, who after having deliberated upon the principles of the order, and binding nature of its obligations, resolved to make a revelation of its mysteries. They confirmed the "ILLUSTRATIONS of Wm. Morgan, published the oaths of twelve degrees of a higher order; appointed a committee to prepare all the degrees which could be obtained for the press; and adjourned to meet on the 4th day of July following.

The committee, with much labor and expense, had all the degrees conferred on a Royal Arch Chapter, Encampment of Knights Templar, and orders of the Holy Cross, ready, and presented them to the convention on the 4th and 5th of July, which declared them correct, an ordered them to be published to the world. The degrees of Mark, Past, and Most Excellent Master, were obtained from Mrs. Morgan, as written by her husband; the Royal Arch, from an agent of the committee, a Royal Arch Mason) as given by Jeremy L. Cross, the Grand Lecturer of the United States; and those of the Encampment and Holy Cross, from a Knight of the Thrice Illustrious Order, as transcribed from a copy as given the Encampment at Le Roy, by the Grand Commander at Utica.

In consequence of the zeal manifested by the fraternity to stifle to excitement, I conceived that much good might be done by a compilation of the most important documents in relation to the subject, By the advice of many friends, and under the patronage of a county and state convention, I undertook the work. While preparing it for the press, I obtained from the 'highest authority' thirty three of the sublime and ineffable degrees, all of which I know to be correct, and I give them to the world "verbatim et literatim." But am I justified in pursuing this course? Will the law of God approve the violation of such solemn oaths? Passing by the arguments which might be adduced from the fact that the obligations were taken without a previous knowledge of their character—the assurances that they were not to interfere with political or religious sentiments, when they were diametrically opposed to both—that I swore fealty to a professedly ancient, moral, benevolent, and righteous institution, when it proves to be "modern corrupt, selfish, and unholy." I rest the question upon the principles of "moral obligation," by which I expect to be judged, and by which must stand or fall. Are the oaths of Free Masonry, then, congenial with the duties which I owe to God and my fellow men? If they are, I most certainly am bound to keep them; if not, to break them. By the principles of moral obligation I am required to promote Gods glory and the best good of the universe. My swearing to love God and my neighbor does not enhance the obligation to all; for it says, "Thou shalt love the Lord thy God with all thy heart and with all thy soul and with all thy strength and with all thy mind, and thy neighbor as thyself." It says this to the sinner and the saint—to the man who has sworn, and to the man who has not sworn, it is infinitely binding on all. It cannot be increased nor diminished—it can require no more—it can receive no less. If I swear to love God and keep his commandments, the oath is binding, because moral obligations made these requisitions before I took the oath, and the oath and the moral obligations are in perfect harmony. If I swear to violate the command of God; for instance, to kill my neighbor, I am bound to break my oath; for the Divine law says, "Thou shalt not kill," and my swearing to violate the command does not, cannot, render to obligation void.—Moral obligation requires me to keep such secrets and such only as are calculated to promote God's glory and the best good of community; and my swearing does not effect the obligation at all. It also requires me to reveal those secrets, the keeping of which have a tendency to mar or prevent His glory and the best good of my neighbor; and my swearing to keep them does not, cannot, render the obligation void; for instance, if I had sworn to keep secret the intention of a highwayman to rob my neighbor's house and murder his family; to keep secret a plot against my country, the government of which is founded upon the principles of truth and justice; to keep secret a grand conspiracy formed by a powerful society, the object of which was, "like that of the Illuminati, to abolish government and social order and extinguish Christianity"—as the keeping of these secrets would be prejudicial to the interests of my neighbor, to the safety of my country, and the glory of God, the principles of moral obligation would require me to reveal them. If I had sworn to assist the robber, to unite in the plot, or conspiracy, my refusing to act in either case, simply, would not fulfill the duties which I should owe to my neighbor, my country, or my God. So I did not make known the intention of the robber, expose the plot, or reveal the conspiracy, I should be guilty of a violation of moral obligation.

It will not be necessary here to inquire whether the oaths to keep the secrets of a brother, with or without exception, to deliver a companion "right or wrong," to "take vengeance on the traitors of Masonry," to "sacrifice all those who reveal the secrets of the order," are in harmony with the Divine law—but whether the principles of moral obligation require the keeping or revealing of Masonic secrets?

It will readily be admitted that the existence of the institution depends upon the keeping of its secrets inviolate. It will follow, then, that if the existence of the institution is necessary, or has a tendency to promote God's glory and the well being of society, the principles of moral obligations require me to keep its secrets, and by revealing them I am guilty of moral perjury! And on the other hand, if the institution is corrupt, has an evil tendency, is opposed to the order and well being of society and the glory of God, I am under moral obligation to break my oaths, and reveal its secrets to the world, that it may come to an end . My refusal to meet with or support the institution is not sufficient, must renounce fealty to the order, reveal its secrets, oppose its influence, and use my exertion to destroy it, or I am guilty of a violation of moral obligation.

Let the reader carefully and thoroughly examine the following documents, and he will discover that Freemasonry, as a system, is dark, unfruitful, selfish, demoralizing, blasphemous, murderous, anti-republican, and anti-Christian—-opposed to the glory of God and the good of mankind; and hence the compiler in bursting asunder the band of the fraternity, and publishing their secrets to the world , is doing no more than is required by the principles of moral obligation--is but fulfilling the duties which he owes to God and his fellow men.

DAVID BERNARD,

Warsaw, April 1, 1829.

The publishing of this book and all the supposed denouncement of Freemasonry, wasn't enough to make the common people buy the Masonic propaganda package. The public outcry against Freemasonry blossomed into a full blown political party called the ANTI-MASONIC PARTY. You may find it surprising that there was such a great public outcry against Freemasonry, and this fact is little known nowadays. It is a part of history that Masonry would just as soon forget. In fact, I see no mention of it in modern history textbooks. Of course there may be some mention of it somewhere, as I haven't read all the modern textbooks, there are. My point is, that nowadays, there is little to no mention of it. And in some of the old history texts which I have read, there is usually only one paragraph which mentions it. Modern encyclopedias do make reference to the Anti-Masonic Party, but that is about all you will find today.

The Anti-Masonic Party claimed many votes in elections of the early 1800's. In the election of 1832, the Anti-Masonic Party was credited with 130,000 votes. At the time, it was fashionable for candidates to claim Anti-Masonic sentiments. John Quincy Adams was one; he talked against Freemasonry. Although, he spoke negatively of it, his political decisions leaned more toward Masonic ideology. John Quincy, was the son of President John Adams, a Mason. Just because a man denounces any Masonic affiliations, does not mean that he is not a Mason. Masonry, at this time, was in big trouble. There were legislative and Senate committees in New York, Massachusetts, and Pennsylvania, during the 1830's, which investigated Masonry. The legislative bodies of these states made many findings against Freemasonry. During the early 1800's, it surely was not in good taste to acknowledge your affiliation with Freemasonry. This is a historical fact. You may question, as I did, how an organization so widespread in high places of government and industry, could or would allow such legislative exposure, without reprisals or a total halt to such legislative diggings. Not all politicians of the 1830's were Masons. Government had spread so fast in the states, that Masonry could not back all elected positions. The secret society could not claim all positions of influence. The same is true today. But, they did not hold positions of the uppermost influence.

Through sheer courage, on the part of some honest politicians, Masonic corruption was finally held accountable. I will now quote from a report of the NEW YORK STATE SENATE COMMITTEE of 1830, on what they found out about Freemasonry...'IT COMPRISES MEN OF RANK, WEALTH, OFFICE AND TALENTS IN POWER... AND THAT ALMOST IN EVERY PLACE WHERE POWER IS OF ANY IMPORTANCE—IT COMPRISES, AMONG THE OTHER CLASSES OF THE COMMUNITY, TO THE LOWEST, IN LARGE NUMBERS, AND CAPABLE OF BEING DIRECTED ,'BY THE EFFORTS OF OTHERS SO AS TO HAVE THE FORCE OF CONCERT THEY THROUGH THE CIVILIZED WORLD!" "THEY ARE DISTRIBUTED TOO, WITH THE MEANS OF KNOWING EACH OTHER, AND THE MEANS OF KEEPING SECRET, AND THE MEANS OF COOPERATING, IN THE DESK, IN THE LEGISLATIVE HALL, ON THE BENCH, IN EVERY GATHERING OF MEN OF BUSINESS, IN EVERY PARTY OF PLEASURE, IN EVERY ENTERPRISE OF GOVERNMENT, IN- EVERY DOMESTIC CIRCLE, IN PEACE AND IN WAR, AMONG ITS ENEMIES AND FRIENDS, IN ONE PLACE AS WELL AS ANOTHER. SO POWERFUL, INDEED, IS IT AT THIS TIME, THAT IT FEARS NOTHING FROM VIOLENCE, EITHER PUBLIC OR PRIVATE, FOR IT HAS EVERY MEANS TO LEARN IT IN SEASON, TO COUNTERACT, DEFEAT AND PUNISH IT..."

The statement also noted, that at the time there were about 30,000 Freemasons in New York State; about one fourth of the voting population. "Yet, they held for forty years," three-fourths of all public offices in the state. This was a powerful statement for the minority of honest politicians to make. At the time, they were literally the mice that roared!" To this very day, the above statements hold true! Nothing has changed, then or now! That statement, and similar ones, made by Massachusetts and Pennsylvania were the last of the truths to about Freemasonry. Their power and their secrecy conquered, even this terrible image. They merely went underground for a while, until things cooled off. The Masonic society survived, intact, and continued launching their barrage of propaganda from their underground stronghold, away from public view, just as the honest politicians had Predicted in their legislative findings.

The few honest, non-Masonic politicians, who did the legislative investigations, know from their findings that Masonic corruption could not be stopped. They knew that their investigations of Freemasonry were an ill-fated attempt, a last stand against evil, so to speak. Personally, I take a non-fatalistic view on the subject of putting an end to this worldwide, sinister plot of world domination. My studies indicate, that although their influence and money can't be rivaled anywhere in the world, (and it is a worldwide secret society,) their plot has an ACHILLES HEEL…. By reading these legislative findings, it is easy to see that this body of non-Masonic politicians had succumbed to Masonry's second line of defense, its struggle for worldwide domination. Masonry's second line of defense is the old tactic of psychological warfare. Their first line of defense is the 25th landmark of secrecy; you are not supposed to know they are running things from behind the scenes.

And in some of the old history texts which I have read, there is usually only one paragraph which mentions it. Modern encyclopedias do make reference to the Anti-Masonic Party, but that is about all you will find today.

The Anti-Masonic Party claimed many votes in elections of the early 1800's. In the election of 1832, the Anti-Masonic Party was credited with 130,000 votes. At the time, it was fashionable for candidates to claim Anti-Masonic sentiments. John Quincy Adams was one; he talked against Freemasonry. Although, he spoke negatively of it, his political decisions leaned more toward Masonic ideology. John Quincy, was the son of President John Adams, a Mason. Just because a man denounces any Masonic affiliations, does not mean that he is not a Mason. Masonry, at this time, was in big trouble. There were legislative and Senate committees in New York, Massachusetts, and Pennsylvania, during the 1830's, which investigated Masonry. The legislative bodies of these states made many findings against Freemasonry. During the early 1800's, it surely was not in good taste to acknowledge your affiliation with Freemasonry. This is a historical fact. You may question, as I did, how an organization so widespread in high places of government and industry, could or would allow such legislative exposure, without reprisals or a total halt to such legislative diggings. Not all politicians of the 1830 's were Masons. Government had spread so fast in the states, that Masonry could not back all elected positions. The secret society could not claim all positions of influence. The same is true today. But, they did not hold positions of the uppermost influence.

If you were to discover the fact that Masonry is running the show, then its second line of defense kicks into gear. With a little digging you expose Masonry's immensity, and when you realize the vast extent of its power, you are supposed to draw the conclusion that Masonry, (the corruption) is invincible. Masonry's tactic, is that once you see their strength you will be scared out of your wits, stopped in your tracks, literally scared speechless. You are supposed to draw the conclusion that you can't fight city hall, and your efforts are supposed to be curtailed at that point. This is always, and I repeat always, the first reaction by people who are exposed to the truths the worldwide rule of the political and religious ideology of Freemasonry. I can quote to you, word for word, and the first utterance of folks who read this book. "So now that I finally know the truth, what the hell can I do about it? It's totally overpowering. And this is the predicted reaction that Freemasonry wants, its second line of defense.

CHAPTER VII

AUTHORS REFLECTIONS

At this point in the book, I feel it necessary to qualify myself, and divulge some of the life experiences which have lead me to the point where I felt, in all conscience, the necessity to write this book. I realize that what I have to say is extremely inflammatory, and it strikes to the core all that many of us, in this country, have held dear for so long. The information I present here is pretty scary stuff. It isn't my intent to scare anyone or to shake anyone's foundations. My only intent, is to present the facts to you, in the hopes that informed people can make changes for the betterment of all, and to answer some questions that loom deeply within most of us. I realize that the things I have to say in this book can be painful, and often times the natural reaction to this sort of pain is denial. (This can't be possible) I derive no joy from writing this book, and I do not expect any monetary gain from it. If I do have monetary gain, it will probably be little to none. Books like this are not allowed to make it to the mainstream public, because the factions I speak of here control a sizeable portion of the publishing industry.

If anything, I risk much by presenting these facts to you. Once I realized the seriousness of what my research had uncovered, I feared to divulge this knowledge to anyone. I feared for my job and my life. Yet, I knew that good, honest, hardworking people should know about what affects their lives in so many important ways. To me, these facts are supremely important. My close associates know but, at one point, and this and family, I decided that I definitely would NOT write this book. My mind was made up that by writing this book, I would put my family and myself in a very risky position.

So, I resolved NOT to do what I knew should be done. My mind was set on keeping my knowledge to myself and go about my life. Then a series of events happened, which, to me, were far beyond coincidence. These events lead me to believe that good conscience and God's will demanded that I write the book in spite of my fears.

My research began strictly as a lark. Personally, I have a curiosity that burns with intensity far beyond the limits of the average man. Simply stated, "I've just always been that way." My curiosity branches out into many areas. I love to study and to learn, yet, I have no college degrees. Unfortunately, in my youth I was quite irresponsible, and viewed school as a great hindrance to my immediate pleasures and pursuits. I did not graduate from high school formally, though I do have an Equivalency Diploma, which I received at about age 25. I did not fully read my first book until age 20. I was a rebellious youth, who resented having a formal education crammed down my throat. Any book reports required by school were made up or taken from inside covers. All this changed as my natural curiosity grew. I became intensely interested in pursuing some subjects such as Anthropology (the study of human cultures, past and present,) Sociology, Nature and Religion, Archeology, Politics, History, and Artistic endeavors, etc., etc., etc. The more I learned, the more I wanted to learn. So, ever since my voluntary introduction to education, in subjects that I was interested in, I have become an eternal student in a wide variety of subjects. The bottomless well of knowledge constantly beckons me into new areas of study.

I once talked to a co-worker about religion and the world situation. He told me he was a member of a benevolent society, which cared much about religion and the state of the world in general. He revealed to me that he was a Mason, and suggested that I would be a good candidate, because I had a religion and cared about the general plight of mankind. I knew nothing about this organization, except for the little signs placed beside the roads outside towns and cities. The signs say, Free and Accepted Masons," with the symbol of the compass, square, and "G." My curiosity was spurred when the co-worker showed me a copy of a Masonic book and told me to look it over. The entire book was written in some form of code, which was unintelligible to me. I asked why this was so and he said, "Freemasonry is not meant to be for all people, just a select few who meet certain requirements." From that point on, I became intensely interested in this organization. I wasn't sure if I wanted to join such a strange group. Besides, I never saw the co-worker again, so I had no way to inquire about joining, even if I decided I wanted to.

A couple of years passed, and one day while taking my refuse to our local landfill, I spotted a black doctor's bag in the landfill, about to be buried. I rescued it to see what might be inside. The bag was intact, I shook it and noticed that there was an object inside. But the bag was locked. I took it home and cut it open. To my amazement, I discovered several untitled books and a Masonic diploma, dated 1925. The books were all written in code, as was the one shown to me by my co-worker, two years before. I was very happy to find these books, because now I would have the opportunity to examine some of this strange literature, at my leisure. My curiosity now raged like an inferno. I longed to know what all this strange hocus pucos was about. I studied and pondered the strange little books, trying to unravel their secrets. I did manage, after a time, to break some of the code, to get a general view of what they were saying. These books contained four different types of code, sometimes used separately and sometimes used together. I gathered that some of these books contained ritual procedures, prayers, allegory, etc., conducted by High Priests, Deacons, and junior Deacons. My curiosity burned, even hotter, this stuff was weird! I spent the next four years, on and off, trying to decode these books.

Then one day, among someone's possessions, I saw a book about Freemasonry. I copied the title, author, and the Library of Congress number. I went to a large local bookstore to place an order for this book. A few weeks later, after not hearing from the bookstore, I went back to inquire about the progress of my order. They informed me that the book did not exist... very strange. I searched every public source for anything I could find on the subject. I ran across a book called, HOLY BLOOD HOLY GRAIL, but I can't remember the name of the author. There was a great deal of information in that book about Masonic history, ideology, and secrets. To this day, I cannot find a copy of this book anywhere. After finding and reading all I could on the subject, fate brought me a new acquaintance. He also, was aware of some of the workings of Freemasonry, and other factions who plotted against the working of Freemasonry, and other factions who plotted against the common people to maintain power. He and I hit it off real well! He had drawn many of the same conclusions I had, from his own research. He introduced me to a little-known publication, which is a clearinghouse for all sorts of literature on secret societies, and many other obscure subjects. I couldn't believe what I had found. Apparently, there is a small faction of folks out there, that don't buy American or World politics at face value. This publisher produces many books on the subject of the inside story on politics and history.

This clearinghouse literature varies from pure racist garbage, to sophisticated literary works on secret societies. I purchased a few books from this source. I was amazed to find there are folks like me, who have made studies of the Freemasons, and gone to great lengths to document their work. I learned much from these authors, often times they verified many of my theories, through their documented research. At times, I realized that I had knowledge of things that their books lacked. Because of the secrecy of Masonic society, and the length of time they have existed, (about 300 years) putting a true picture of them together is like trying to assemble a giant jigsaw puzzle; not all of us have access to all the pieces. I can safely say, after viewing the puzzle that I have assembled, that I now have about 90 percent of the pieces. The other 10 percent are lost in time and secrecy. I strongly felt that what I had uncovered was important for others to know. Hence, this book, and the overcoming of my fear about writing it.

CHAPTER VIII

DEMOCRACY AND DEPOTISM

In the beginning of this book I raised some issues as food for thought. I also raised questions of why our government, at first glance seemed democratic, but upon close examination reveals itself, in actuality, to be despotic. I now intend to answer these questions and give some insight into the mindset of the forefathers who contrived this government and their reason for doing so.

First, let's look at the dictionary definitions of DEMOCRACY and DESPOTISM, so as to clarify in our minds the distinction between the two, and to make more obvious the points I intend to set forth. Webster's definition of DESPOT, "AN ABSOLUTE RULER (generally in a bad sense); A TYRANT." DEMOCRACY, A FORM OF GOVERNMENT IN WHICH THE SUPREME POWER IS VESTED IN THE PEOPLE." The Webster definition of TYRANT is, "A CRUEL SOVEREIGN OR MASTER, OPPRESSOR." If you remove the word "tyrant" out of "despotism," you basically have, "benevolent despotism." Although a despot is still an oppressing force," even though he may not be a tyrant, I maintain that by reading the rules, (the Constitution) and reading them thoroughly, without reading anything into them, that you find we are ruled by a despotic form of government... sold to the people under the guise of democracy. I use the word, "guise," because the people are supposed to be the "supreme power," but obviously are not. In a democracy, the people choose their leader.

Because of the Electoral College, the people don't choose their main leader, the president. There is some further clarification needed here on the subject of democracy. All U.S. officials in government will readily admit that we don't have a true democracy in the U.S., and that because democracy has some drawbacks, we really would not want a true democracy running our country. In a true democracy, the peoples' rule is supreme. Majority rules. The following scenario can easily illustrate the main drawback with a true democracy. In a true democracy, if the majority of the people voted to kill all homosexuals because the majority thought them strange, and their presence was unwanted by the majority... then all homosexuals would have to be done away with. So, in a sense, a true democracy is not the most desirable, practical, or humanistic form of government. With this last statement, I totally agree. My problem is that the forefathers, the framers of the Constitution used the easily cured flaw in democracy, as an excuse to swing the governmental rule back towards despotism, under the guise of democracy. They used the easily curable flaw in democracy as an excuse to institute an Electoral College, which nullifies the popular vote. This easily curable flaw in democracy could be attended to by a board of human rights, which basically we already have. We have people assigned to settle human rights issues. This flaw was just an excuse to steal power from the people. I will now quote from a 1968 history textbook called, "AMERICAN HISTORY REVIEW TEXT" by IRVING L. GORDON: Paragraph title, "UNDEMOCRATIC FEATURES IN THE ORIGINAL CONSTITUTION," (THE CONSTITUTION BEFORE THE INSISTENCE OF THE BILL OF RIGHTS.) "MANY OF THE FOUNDING FATHERS FEARED WHAT THEY CALLED "EXCESS" OF DEMOCRACY. CONSEQUENTLY, THEY INCLUDED IN THE ORIGINAL CONSTITUTION SEVERAL PROVISIONS LIMITING THE POWER OF THE PEOPLE. (1) THE CONSTITUTION PROVIDES FOR THE ELECTION OF THE PRESIDENT, NOT BY THE PEOPLE, BUT BY AN ELECTORAL COLLEGE. IN MANY STATES, THE ELECTORS WERE ORIGINALLY CHOSEN BY THE STATE LEGISLATURES. (2) THE ORIGINAL CONSTITUTION PROVIDED FOR THE ELECTION OF UNITED STATES SENATORS, NOT DIRECTLY BY THE PEOPLE, BUT BY THE STATE LEGISLATURES. (3) THE ORIGINAL CONSTITUTION

LEFT TO THE STATES THE POWER TO DETERMINE WHO SHALL VOTE. IT CONTAINED NO PROVISION OUTLAWING PROPERTY OR RELIGIOUS QUALIFICATION FOR VOTING AND NO PROVISION GRANTING VOTING RIGHTS TO WOMEN. FURTHERMORE, THE ORIGINAL CONSTITUTION ACCEPTANCE AND PROTECTED THE UNDEMOCRATIC INSTITUTION OF SLAVERY."

What does the fear of excess of democracy have to do with who will choose the President? There is no justification or rational to take this right away from the people in choosing their president. The one flaw, as I said, could easily be cured by human rights people. By the way, the other flaw in excesses of democracy is the excuse by our forefathers, that the people may not know what is good for them. So, we need a governing body that can make decisions for us. So as a result, they take away our right to choose our leaders. CUTE! REAL CUTE! The forefathers, the rich elite, and Masonic ruling class, couldn't have cared less about democracy. It is quite obvious when you study the Constitution they wrote up, which excluded a Bill of Rights. Remember, I said the Bill of Rights was thrown in as a bone for the peasants, when they became outraged upon finding out about this Constitution. Strictly a "LET THEM EAT CAKE" attitude. Masons are against all forms of despotism, except their own form. They believe in the ruling class and the worker class, and that God left them, the Masons, in charge of running the world, because of their superior intellect. Remember the back of the dollar bill? "ANNUIT CCEPTIS" ... He (God) approves of our undertaking. Apparently, as far as Masonic ideology is concerned, God approves of all their bullshit!

Now I will illustrate how intent these Masonic masters were in gaining control and robbing the people of their rights. I quote from IRVING L. GORDON'S HISTORY REVIEW TEXT, again, "THE DELEGATES DISAGREED OVER THE TERM OF OFFICE OF THE PRESIDENT AND THE METHOD OF CHOOSING HIM. SUGGESTIONS FOR HIS TERM OF OFFICE RANGED FROM THREE YEARS TO LIFE. (LIFE? Where were these peoples' heads at?) SOME DELEGATES WANTED THE PRESIDENT

ELECTED DIRECTLY BY THE PEOPLE. OTHERS, FEARING TOO MUCH DEMOCRACY, SUGGESTED THAT HE BE ELECTED BY CONGRESS. THE ISSUES WERE SETTLED (A) BY AUTHORIZING A TENURE OF FOUR YEARS, AND (B) BY ESTABLISHING A COMPLEX PROCEDURE FOR ELECTING THE PRESIDENT, THROUGH AN ELECTORAL COLLEGE OR, IF NO CANDIDATE RECEIVED A MAJORITY IN THE ELECTORAL COLLEGE, THROUGH THE HOUSE OF REPRESENTATIVES. BY THIS PROCEDURE, THE DELEGATES MEANT TO ALLOW THE PEOPLE ONLY AN INDIRECT VOICE IN CHOOSING THE PRESIDENT"

The framers of the Constitution were intensely concerned with who chooses the president. Above all else they had to ensure that a Mason became president. And the only way to do that was to cheat the people out of their choice through an elaborate system called the Electoral College. Remember? I said that the Electoral College is the first thing mentioned in the Constitution. Peoples' cares and concerns, when put in writing, are usually placed in a position of priority in a document. In other words, things that bother people most, is what you see first.

THE CONSTITUTION OF THE UNITED STATES... Article 1, Section 2... THE HOUSE OF REPRESENTATIVES SHALL BE COMPOSED OF MEMBERS CHOSEN EVERY SECOND YEAR BY THE PEOPLE OF THE SEVERAL STATES, AND THE ELECTORS IN EACH STATE SHALL HAVE THE QUALIFICATIONS REQUISITE FOR ELECTORS OF THE MOST NUMEROUS BRANCH OF STATE LEGISLATURE. (What qualifications are required of these electors, that they be Masons?) The Constitution's only qualification for elector is that they don't hold an office of trust or profit under the United States. All others such as the president, vice-president, and senator qualifications are very specific. The Constitution also called for senators to be chosen by the legislature, not the people. But later on, the people were so angry with this, that the leaders added the 17th Amendment to the Constitution giving the people the right to choose their senators by popular vote. The rulers gave in grudgingly to the demand... but not until 1913. Talk about stacking the deck!

Article2, Section 1, Paragraph 2; EACH STATE SHALL APPOINT IN SUCH MANNER AS THE LEGISLATURE THEREOF MAY DIRECT A NUMBER OF ELECTORS, EQUAL TO THE WHOLE NUMBER OF SENATORS AND REPRESENTATIVES TO WHICH THE STATE MAY BE ENTITLED IN CONGRESS: BUT NO SENATOR OR REPRESENTATIVE, OR PERSON HOLDING AN OFFICE OF TRUST OR PROFIT UNDER THE UNITED STATES, SHALL BE APPOINTED AN ELECTOR. (Note: they state these electors will be appointed, not elected.) VOTE SHALL MEET IN THEIR RESPECTIVE STATES, AND VOTE BY BALLOT FOR TWO PERSONS, OF WHOM ONE AT LEAST SHALL NOT BE AN INHABITANT OF THE SAME STATE WITH THEMSELVES. AND THEY SHALL MAKE A LIST OF ALL THE PERSONS VOTED FOR, AND OF THE NUMBER VOTES FOR EACH: WHICH LIST THEY SHALL SIGN AND CERTIFY AND TRANSMIT SEALED TO THE SEAT OF GOVERNMENT OF THE UNITED STATES, DIRECTED TO THE PRESIDENT OF THE SENATE. THE PRESIDENT OF THE SENATES SHALL, IN THE PRESIDENT OF THE SENATE SHALL, IN THE PRESENCE OF THE SENATE AND HOUSE OF REPRESENTATIVE, OPEN ALL THE CERTIFICATES, AND THE VOTES SHALL THEN BE COUNTED. THE PERSON HAVING THE GREATEST NUMBER BE A MAJORITY OF THE WHOLE NUMBER OF ELECTION APPOINTED; AND IF THERE BE MORE THAN ONE WHO HAVE SUCH MAJORITY, AND HAVE AN EQUAL NUMBERS OF VOTES, THEN THE HOUSE OF REPRESENTATIVES SHALL IMMEDIATELY CHOOSE BY BALLOT ONE OF THEM FOR PRESIDENT; AND IF NO PERSON HAVE A MAJORITY, THEN FROM THE FIVE HIGHEST ON THE LIST THE SAID HOUSE SHALL IN LIKE A MANNER CHOOSE THE PRESIDENT. (Are you with me so far? Yeah, you and a Philadelphia lawyer) BUT IN CHOOSING THE PRESIDENT, THE VOTES SHALL BE TAKEN BY STATES, THE REPRESENTATION FROM EACH STATE HAVING ONE VOTE; A QUORUM FOR THIS PURPOSE SHALLL CONSIST OF A MEMBER OR MEMBERS FROM

TWO-THIRDS OF THE STATES, AND A MAJORITY OF ALL THE STATES SHALL BE NECESSARY TO CHOICE. IN EVERY CASE, AFTER THE CHOICE OF PRESIDENT, THE PERSON HAVING THE GREATEST NUMBER OF VOTES OF ELECTORS SHALL BE THE VICE-PRESIDENT BUT IF THERE SHOULD REMAIN TWO OR MORE WHO HAVE EQUAL VOTES, THE SENATE SHALL CHOOSE FROM THEM BY BALLOT THE VICE-PRESIDENT. Paragraph 3; THE CONGRESS MAY DETERMINE THE TIME OF CHOOSING THE ELECTORS, AND THE DAY ON WHICH THEY SHALL GIVE THEIR VOTES; WHICH DAY SH ALL BE THE SAME THROUGHOUT THE UNITED STATES.

The 23 amendments gave the District of Columbia 3 electoral votes even though it is not a state. Let's make damn sure the ceck is stacked properly here folks. Can you see why the common people thought our Constitution to be purposefully confusing? Can you now begin to see how concerned, and to what lengths, they went to steal the peoples' vote? I stated previously that the Electoral College was the main tool enacted into constitutional law, which is utilized to nullify the peoples' vote. It is a little known, and totally unpublished fact, that the Electoral College has actually on three occasions nullified the popular vote. I will now list three elections where the Electoral College was utilized for their ultimate purpose.

1... JOHN QUINCY ADAMS IN THE ELECTION OF 1824, FIRST PRESIDENT ELECTED WITHOUT RECEIVING PLURALITY OF EITHER THE ELECTORAL COLLEGE OR POPULAR VOTE. HE RAN AGAINST ANDREW JACKSON; JACKSON RECEIVED 153,544 POPULAR VOTES AND ADAMS RECEIVED 108,740. Even the Electoral College screwed up on this one, and couldn't get a majority, so the House of Representatives did the choosing in accordance with the Constitution. ADAMS WAS CHOSEN AGAINST POPULAR VOTE. In the election of 1888, Grover Cleveland ran against Benjamin Harrison. Cleveland received 5,556,918 popular votes; Harrison received 5,176,108. The Electoral College blatantly went against the people and put Harrison in the president's seat. # 3... IN THE ELECTION OF 1876, TILDEN RAN AGAINST HAYES. TILDEN RECEIVED 4,300,590 VOTES

AND HAYES RECEIVED 4,036,298 POPULAR VOTES. AGAIN, THE ELECTORAL COLLEGE WENT AGAINST THE PEOPLES WISHES.

The above facts were taken from the book called, "FACTS ABOUT THE PRESIDENTS," by NATHAN KANE, published by; H. W. WILSON. N.Y., N.Y. 1973. "OF THE PEOPLE, BY THE PEOPLE, FOR THE PEOPLE" was the propaganda cry of our forefathers. This was the cry the people were supposed to "buy." Of course, most people still believe our forefathers really meant it. Why did our forefathers make the Electoral College law if they really believed the government was supposed to be for the people? Why did they go to such lengths to enact the Electoral College? It should be obvious now why they went to great lengths to keep control of the vote. Obviously, they never meant for the people to have the final say. Surely, the ruling elite would not turn over the power to the people, to choose a president; unless it was for a good reason or to prove a point... I am not certain whether or not JOHN F. KENNEDY was a Mason, but I think the Masons had to convince the Catholic, that even they had say in running things... until J.F.K. had outlived his usefulness.

Can you now see why PATRICK HENRY was pissed? These Masonic forefathers were going to make sure their man got in. Then there is Article 12, which is another long dissertation on a change of the Electoral College, which states in brief, "ELECTORS SHALL CAST SEPARATE BALLOTS FOR PRESIDENT AND VICE-PRESIDENT 1801." And unfortunately, this same garbage exists today. The Electoral College is still in operation, and the Masons own all the horses in the race, whether Republican, Democrat, or Independent.

CHAPTER IX

MORE CONSTITUTIONAL BACKGROUND

If you are an ex-serviceman, this is the kind of stuff you swore to uphold. Another quote from IRVING L. GORDON: 1968 Review Text in American History titled, "CONSTITUTIONAL CONVENTION AT PHILADELPHIA (1787) #2 ABSENTEES, "THE PHILADELPHIA CONVENTION INCLUDED SCARCELY ANY REPRESENTATIVES OF SMALL FARMERS, CITY WORKERS, AND FRONTIERSMEN, ALTHOUGH THESE GROUPS TOTALED OVER 90 PERCENT OF THE COUNTRY'S POPULATION." (90 percent, folks!) #3 DELEGATES, "THE PHILADELPHIA CONVENTION CONSISTED OF 55 DELEGATES FROM ALL THE STATES, EXCEPT RHODE ISLAND. (I should think that attendance by all the states would be necessary to draw up such an important document.) "SINCE THEY WERE MAINLY LAWYERS, LARGE LANDOWNERS, BANKERS, AND MERCHANTS, THEY REFLECTED PROPERTIED AND BUSINESS INTERESTS." (Surely nothing has changed today, and all this, remember, was supposed to be for the people.) "THEY WERE WELL EDUCATED MEN, WHO HAD READ WIDELY IN HISTORY, GOVERNMENT AND LAW. THEY WERE ESPECIALLY FAMILIAR WITH ENGLAND'S PROGRESS TOWARDS DEMOCRACY AND WITH THE IDEAS OF GREAT POLITICAL PHILOSOPHERS, SUCH AS LOCKE AND MONTESQUIEU. MOREOVER, MANY DELEGATES HAD PRACTICAL EXPERIENCE IN POLITICS, HAVING SERVED AS GOVERNORS, JUDGES, AND LEGISLATORS." Oh yes, surely we know what is best for the people... Another quote from IRVING L. GORDON; #2, "DEBATE OVER RATIFICATION.

THE FEDERALISTS, SUPPORTERS OF THE CONSTITUTION, CONSISTED OF MEN WITH BUSINESS AND PROPERTY INTERESTS, AND OF OTHERS WHO CONSIDERED THE NATION MORE IMPORTANT THAN THEIR STATES." (I would like to rephrase the last sentence... WHO CARED MORE ABOUT LINING THEIR POCKETS INSTEAD OF BOLSTERING JUSTICE. As you well know, big business does not care one iota about nationalism or patriotic ideas. Big business has no morals and owes no allegiance to the country, let alone its people. Big business always goes where the money is, and they don't care whose people they sell out to.

"THEY ARGUED THAT THE CONSTITUTION WOULD PROVIDE A STABLE GOVERNMENT CAPABLE OF MAIN TAINING LAW AND ORDER." Oh yes, a very stable government with no revolts by the people to interfere with the accumulation of money and power. Remember the all seeing eye and pyramid on the back of the one dollar bill is a Masonic symbol of economic stability, no revolts, capable of maintaining law and order, oh yeah! Right! Like we have so much law and order today. Right! "FURTHERING ECONOMIC PROSPERITY, AND COMMANDING RESPECT ABROAD. THE ANTI-FEDERALIST OPPONENTS OF THE CONSTITUTION CONSISTED OF FARMERS, CITY WORKERS AND OTHERS WHO GAVE THEIR CHIEF LOYALTY TO THEIR STATE OR COMMUNITY. THEY ARGUED THAT THE CONSTITUTION SERVES THE PROPERTIED CLASSES, THREATENED THE POWERS OF STATES, AND LEFT PEOPLE UNPROTECTED AGAINST FEDERAL ENCROACHMENT UPON THEIR CIVIL LIBERTIES. ACKNOWLEDGING THE LAST ARGUMENT, THE FEDERALISTS PLEDGED TO ADD A BILL OF RIGHTS TO THE CONSTITUTION."

Yes, they added a Bill of Rights to the Constitution, but their original intention was just the Constitution without a Bill of Rights. (This typifies the mind-set of the forefathers, they were elitist Masons, and surely did not have the peoples' best interest in mind. Remember, the Bill of Rights was grudgingly thrown in because of public outcry, not because of the founders' benevolence.

IRVING L. GORDON, again, "REASONS FOR THE SUCCESS OF THE FEDERALISTS (A), A WELL ORGANIZED GROUP, THE FEDERALISTS EXPENDED MUCH ENERGY AND MONEY TOWARD ACHIEVING RATIFICATION. AT VARIOUS STATE RATIFYING CONVENTIONS, THE FEDERALISTS WON THE SUPPORT OF DOUBTFUL DELEGATES AND DELAYED THE VOTING UNTIL THEY WERE ASSURED A MAJORITY. THE ANTI-FEDERALISTS COULD NOT COMPARE WITH THEM IN FUNDS, ORGANIZATION, AND EFFECTIVENESS. THE ANTIFEDERALISTS WERE FURTHER HANDICAPPED BY THE FACT THAT THEY WERE SUPPORTING THE WEAK (or so called weak) ARTICLES OF THE CONFEDERATION." (B) MOST SUPPORTERS OF RATIFICATION COULD SATISFY STATE PROPERTY QUALIFICATIONS FOR VOTING AND COULD THEREFORE VOTE FOR CONVENTION DELEGATES. THE ANTI-FEDERALIST URBAN WORKERS AND POOR PEOPLE, PROBABLY ONE THIRD OF THE POPULATION, LACKED PROPERTY AND WERE DENIED THE VOTE."

Let's not forget, at that time states had requirements which demanded that you had to own property to be able to vote. So elitist ideology was at work within the states themselves. The picture emerges now, of the elitist rule and elitist ideology at the root of our country's beginning and is prevalent throughout its history. The people who made up 90% of the population, the people who were supposed to be the ones who benefited from all this, never had a chance. "OF THE PEOPLE, BY THE PEOPLE, FOR THE PEOPLE." Give me a break, folks! The anti-federalists weren't buying it, and I don't buy it.

IRVING L. GORDON again (D) "THE FEDERALISTS ENJOYED THE SUPPORT OF TWO HIGHLY RESPECTED MEN, BENJAMIN FRANKLIN AND GEORGE WASHINGTON. THEIR APPROVAL OF THE CONSTITUTION INFLUENCED MANY DOUBTERS." Benjamin Franklin and George Washington, two all time great Masons... two provable Masons.

Now, I want to bring your attention to the constitutional abilities of the people to change their government, and what the forefathers had to say on the subject. I will get back to the issue of the Electoral College shortly, because there is more proof that I want to bring forth about it. But at this time I feel it necessary to illustrate more fully what the forefathers said about governmental change, and what they actually wrote down as law into our Constitution. As is always and I repeat, as always is the case, our Masonic politicians make great promises and speak with silver tongues; but never produce anything near what they have promised, in actual policy making. My premise is that this political propagandizing has gone on since the beginning and is nothing new. I now quote a passage written by THOMAS JEFFERSON in his effort to sell the people a bill of goods. IRVING L. GORDON 1968, "PHILOSOPHY OF GOVERNMENT, THOMAS JEFFERSON (A) "ALL MEN ARE CREATED EQUAL" (except for slaves and non-propertied people) and "ARE ENDOWED BY THEIR CREATOR WITH CERTAIN INALIENABLE RIGHTS" including "LIFE, LIBERTY, AND THE PURSUIT OF HAPPINESS." (B) "TO SECURE THESE RIGHTS, THE GOVERNMENT HAS INSTITUTED AMONG MEN, DERIVING THEIR JUST POWERS FROM THE CONSENT OF THE GOVERNED." (C) "WHENEVER ANY FORM OF GOVERNMENT BECOMES DESTRUCTIVE OF THESE ENDS, IT IS THE RIGHT OF THE PEOPLE TO ALTER, TO ABOLISH IT, AND TO INSTITUTE NEW GOVERNMENT." All this sounds great, doesn't it? These are the kinds of silver-tongued speeches that all these Masonic forefathers were spewing out for the people to hear, not only at that time, but also today. Now let me quote to you from the Constitution, what these men made into law. They say one thing, then turn around and make laws that say the opposite. They justified their reasons for starting a bloody revolt against England, in the Declaration of Independence, but this is the law they gave to the people to change their government, if necessary. Article I, Section 8, Paragraph 15; TO PROVIDE FOR CALLING FORTH THE MILITIA TO EXECUTE THE LAWS OF THE UNION, SUPPRESS INSURRECTIONS AND REPEL INVASIONS." Article I, Section 9, Paragraph 2; "THE PRIVILEGE OF THE WRIT OF HABEAS CORPUS SHALL NOT BE SUSPENDED, UNLESS WHEN IN CASE OF REBELLION OR INVASION THE

PUBLIC SAFETY MAY REQUIRE IT." Article I of the BILL OF RIGHTS, "CONGRESS SHALL MAKE NO LAW RESPECTING AN ESTABLISHMENT OF RELIGION OR PROHIBITING THE FREE EXERCISE THEREOF: (I guess they have held true to this part, there is no law saying that you must join the Masonic religion.) OR ABRIDGING THE FREEDOM OF SPEECH, OR OF THE PRESS: OR THE RIGHT OF THE PEOPLE PEACEFULLY TO ASSEMBLE, AND TO PETITION THE GOVERNMENT FOR A REDRESS OF GRIEVANCES." Big talk by Jefferson, little action stated in Constitutional law. By the way, it is verified that Jefferson was a Mason, benevolent guy that he was. Also, the property restrictions on voting were not fully removed until 1828.

Okay, on with the Electoral College. Here is another quote from, IRVING L. GORDON, 1968 edition of AMERICAN HISTORY REVIEW TEXT. "3 FROM UNDEMOCRATIC INTENT TO RUBBER STAMP." THE FOUNDING FATHERS DEVISED THE ELECTORAL SYSTEM SO AS TO REDUCE (or nullify) THE VOICE OF THE LANDHOLDING PEOPLE IN ELECTING THE PRESIDENT. THEY INTENDED THAT THE ELECTORS EXPRESS THEIR OWN JUDGEMENT. (What about the peoples' judgment? Those dear people so highly spoken of by men of Freemasonry; Washington, Jefferson, Adams, Franklin, etc.) SINCE 1796, HOWEVER, POLITICAL PARTIES HAVE OVERCOME THIS UNDEMOCRATIC INTENT BY NAMING ELECTORS WHO WERE PLEDGED IN ADVANCE TO VOTE FOR THE PARTY'S PRESIDENTIAL CANDIDATE. THUS, THE PEOPLE VOTE FOR THE PRESIDENTIAL CANDIDATE THEY DESIRE BY VOTING FOR HIS GROUP OF ELECTORS, AND THE ELECTORAL COLLEGE REFLECTS THE PEOPLES' WISHES. IT HAS BECOME A RUBBER STAMP," I. L. Gordon was correct when he said "the undemocratic intent." But, he was definitely wrong in his statement that political parties have overcome this "undemocratic intent" by means of the rubber stamp effect. I will prove beyond any doubt that there is NO way to overcome the undemocratic effects of the Electoral College, not by the rubber stamp or anything else. It is historical fact, that on several occasions the Electoral College has gone against the popular vote. So after reading some quotes from an ordinary American History Text Book from 1968, you see that Mr. Gordon sort of tries to tell what actually happened in our history. But when he speaks about things that are totally contrary to democracy, he tries to cover up undemocratic practices by stating that the problem was rectified in favor of the people, which they were not.

Anyway, why were our founding fathers putting forth undemocratic laws when they constantly preached democracy? It should be quite obvious by now, that our founding fathers were a bunch of Masonic, two-faced, silver-tongued devils. There is no other description of them, and in all reality, there could be no other. The undemocratic practices, policymaking, and lies perpetuated by our past and present political deities are food for several books. I have given only a few examples, such as Alien Sedition Act, Justice Hugo Black, etc. I will now quote a book I found on the past presidents of the United States. The book, "ATLAS OF THE PRESIDENTS" by DONALD E. COOKE, is copyrighted 1964, 1967, and 1971. It contained, along with the book, a chart of the presidents and a brief description about the Electoral College. The book gives a concise run down of all the presidents, up to Nixon, plus a breakdown of both popular and Electoral votes for each president, except for the first four elected presidents. Anyway, here is what the book says about the Electoral College, "STRANGE AS IT MAY SEEM, IT IS POSSIBLE FOR A CANDIDATE TO RECEIVE A MAJORITY OF POPULAR VOTES AND STILL LOSE THE ELECTION, BECAUSE ANOTHER CANDIDATE MAY RECEIVE A MAJORITY OF ELECTORAL VOTES. IN FACT, BOTH PRESIDENT HAYES IN 1876 AND PRESIDENT HARRISON IN 1888 WERE ELECTED ALTHOUGH THEY RECEIVED FEWER POPULAR VOTES THAN THEIR OPPONENTS." My point is, that the Constitution, its Electoral College, and all the other legal rhetoric in it, was and is a plot fulfilled and operating against the people. And I believe, I have proved beyond a reasonable doubt that my assertions are correct.

Surely, this book is not capable of conveying all the information that is available on the subject of Masonic placement in World

History. The subject is vast and because of secrecy, the information is very difficult to find. Information on worldwide Masonic political activity is not in history books. It must be dug for in the Library of Congress, and in secret Masonic literature, which is anything except accessible to the public. I can assure that some information will never come to light of day. For anyone who is interested in delving into other aspects of Masonic politics and their world influence, you must read other authors who have dug in a wider range of areas than I have. For the purpose of this book, I have concentrated my efforts in one corner of Free Masonic influence, that is, early American constitutional influence and its effect on American freedom as a whole. I suggest that if you intend to become a serious student and desire further proof, PAUL A. FISHER'S book, "BEHIND THE LODGE DOOR," is required reading. Published by TAN BOOKS AND PUBLISHERS, INC., P.O. BOX 424, ROCKFORD, ILLINOIS 61105, LIBRARY OF CONGRESS # 93-61894, ISBN 0-89555-455-0. Mr. Fisher provides a whole roster of important names of people who run the country, and who are members of Masonry. His research is extensive. My basic premise is only the fact that this country's government is not what it appears to be and never was. Also, that the people have been plotted against from the beginning. And, that because of this plot, the people have suffered innumerable hardships, such as dying in wars started by the rich elitists, to line their own pockets... not to mention taxes beyond all reason.

CHAPTER X

MINIMUM SLAVE WAGES

The men who founded this country and the men who contrived to turn it, have pissed away our tax dollars faster than they can steal them from us. Instead of insuring freedom and the pursuit of happiness for the people, they have slapped shackles on all our legs and necks. Do you think that slavery was abolished by the 13th Amendment of the Constitution? On paper it was abolished. In reality, slavery is alive and kicking, in the U.S., as well as other countries today. You may say this statement of mine is totally absurd, but if you think about it carefully, you will realize that this statement makes a lot of sense. Back when George Bush was president, he vetoed to raise the minimum wage from $3.85 per hour to $4.25 per hour, twice. Finally, his bosses, who thought it was time to throw another bone to the peasants, overrode Bush's insistence, and the $4.25 per hour wage was instituted.

Most folks probably didn't realize it but, the U.S. was the last, supposedly progressive, industrialized nation to abolish child labor in 1911. But it wasn't totally dealt with until 1933. Is a person who makes $4.25 per hour any better off than a slave? And, is a man who would veto a raise from $3.85 per hour any better than a slave master? We know George Bush is a Mason. We know that most of these forefathers, at least the important ones, were Masons. We know they advocated slavery in spite of their political rhetoric to the contrary. We know that Jefferson placed a clause in his last will and testament to free his slaves upon his death. Was it because of his benevolence or because it would make his historical image look better? Note that his will stated that they be freed after his death. Possibly, he realized that slaves aren't very useful in the hereafter!

So, do you think a person who tries to exist on $4.25 per hour has a better form of existence than a slave even if he or she is single? Certainly not. Do you think a person making $8.00 per hour, with a family of three or four is any better off than a slave? Do you think their anxieties are any less than a slave's? Picture living on $8.00 per hour, your car is falling apart, constantly breaking down when you are on important missions, the kids are in constant need of shoes, etc., you eat spaghetti three times a week, and you don't have a medical plan. I believe this person's anxiety level is greater than that of slaves. The master had to provide food, clothing, shelter, and some medical attention; else his slaves couldn't produce for him. Even if the free person earns $13.00 per hour, they are still going to work until they have one foot in the grave. They will never get ahead, because the cost of living, controlled by the powers that be, goes up faster than any increase in wages. Did these Masonic forefathers truly have compassion for the people? Surely, they did not. We were and still are only a means to their end. Yes, the forefathers were faced with a difficult task... How do we control the slaves and convince them that they aren't slaves? They accomplished this task beautifully through planned propaganda and vast patronage. There are millions of Masons in this country today. Not all Masonic members are guilty of purposeful plotting, and most reap no great benefits from membership in the fraternity. At best, most of the main body of Masonry reap only the benefits of fraternity, admittance into Masonic Old Age Homes, and satisfaction in affiliation with an organization which appears to do good.

One example of doing good would be the Shriners Burn Hospital. (Shriners are men who have reached the 32nd degree in Masonry.) Other examples are charity work, the Shrine Circus, and Masonic Disease Research, which Masonry does do. Most Masons aren't fully aware of the workings of the Masonic elite, that is the 33rd degree, the members of the C.F.R. (Council of Foreign Relations, or the Bildibergers). The 33rd degree of Masonry is attained only by a minute fraction of the most powerful men in the world, plus a few token common 33rds. Masons in the lower degrees are duped into believing they are entrusted with important secrets, but it is admitted by ALBERT PIKE in MORALS AND DOGMA, that this is purposefully deceitful. "IT IS NOT INTENDED THAT MASONS IN THE BLUE DEGREES SHALL UNDERSTAND THEM, BUT IT IS INTENDED THAT (THEY) SHALL IMAGINE THEY DO. THE TRUE EXPLANATIONS OF THE SYMBOLS ARE RESERVED FOR THE ADEPTS, THE PRINCES OF MASONRY." Masons are also lead to believe that the true adepts are centered within the higher degrees, so when a man reaches the 32nd degree, he feels he knows most of what Masonry has to offer, but he is sadly mistaken.

A quote from A. E. WHITE, from his essay called, AN INTRODUCTION TO C.B.C.S.-(the C.B.C.S. is coded... which I decoded into Christian Brothers and Christian Sisters) IT IS AN EXCELLENT AND INCONTROVERTIBLE TRUTH THAT AS ANGLE OF NINETY DEGREES IS THE FOURTH PART OF A CIRCLE, BUT A STORY ILLUSTRATING THIS ELEMENTARY FACT OF GEOMETRY BELONGS TO THE REGION OF TRIVIA: THE ADMITTED CODE OF ETHICS IS ALSO EXCELLENT AND INCONTESTABLE, BUT IT DOES NOT LEND ITSELF TO SYMBOLISM AND IF WE FIND IN THE MASONIC SYMBOLISM MUCH WHICH IS UNEXPLAINABLE BY ELEMENTARY GEOMETRY OR BY THE COMMON MAXIMS OF MORALITY WE HAVE THE RIGHT TO LOOK FURTHER AND EVERY STUDENT OF THE FRATERNITY WILL BE JUSTIFIED AT ONCE BY THE HAUNTING SENSE THAT THROUGHOUT ITS MODERN RITUALS THERE ARE CERTAIN AFFILIATIONS WHICH TAKE US BACK THROUGH ALL THE CHRISTIAN CENTURIES, EVEN TO ELEUSIS AND TO EGYPT. THE MYSTERY SURROUNDING THESE ELEMENTS CONSTITUTES IN THESE DAYS THE ONLY REAL SECRET OF MASONRY; EXCEPT INDEED THE RISE AND ORIGIN OF THE SYMBOLIC CRAFT ITSELF (the craft is another name for Freemasonry) BUT THIS IS ANOTHER ASPECT OF THE SAME MYSTERY. IT IS THEREFORE TRUE TO SAY THAT THE MASONIC SECRET IS NOT TAUGHT IN LODGES OR IN ANY MANNER COMMUNICATED FOR INITIATES BUT IS DISCOVERED, IF IT IS EVER DISCOVERED, BY THE INITIATE FOR HIMSELF AND THAT THIS BEING SO

THE ADEPTS IN MASONRY ARE EXCEEDINGLY FEW, THAT IS THOSE WHO ARE ADMITTED TO THE ADEPTA, (adepta, The most supreme knowledge in Masonry, understanding all the secrets.) THOUGH THE POSTULANTS AT THE THRESHOLD ARE INNUMERABLE." That is correct, many reach the 32nd degree and are on the threshold, but never really know the secrets.

A quote by A. E. WHITE, from the Masonic magazine called, THE BUILDER": "THE ARTS AND MYSTERIES WHICH WE ARE PLEDGED TO CONCEAL FROM THE PROFANE ARE ALSO THOSE OF THE PECULIAR LAW OF LIFE IN MASONRY BY WHICH THE ENDS CAN BE REACHED." The profane are all the people not associated with Masonry. Not a very nice way to refer to people outside the fraternity. Also judging by the statement, previous to this one, they don't think much of their own members who, they may be Masons all their lives, never really know the promised secrets. Are they also considered profane? Of course, they are just dues payers and workers.

Thirty second-degree Masons are common, they are many and they know little more of the truths than the entering apprentice Mason. The true story isn't totally revealed until a man reaches the 33rd degree. The 33rd degrees are truly the kings of the world. At the 32nd degree you have a pretty good idea of what is going on in Masonry. The top degree, the supreme council of the 33rd degree, is not attainable by ordinary Masons. This degree is reserved for the most powerful and the richest of the rich. Basically, most Masons in the organization are just dues payers. As far as their charitable work goes, even the Mafia goes to church on Sunday and contributes to charities. You may ask, how can a man be tempted to join such an organization? It's really quite simple, man, by himself feels insignificant and powerless. If he can be affiliated with an entity larger than himself, he feels more significant. If the entity or organization is rich and widespread, man feels like he has some power, some say so in his life. Then you add the fact that Freemasonry is a worldwide, supposedly benevolent organization, with many famous members, past and present, you have an organization that is very attractive to men seeking the attributes thereof. Not only that, but it is a noted "old boy network." This being so, there could be monetary advantage in joining. The idea that so many famous men have been members is attractive enough. The idea is that if, Freemasonry is good for all these famous people, then it couldn't possibly be bad for me. Besides, look at all the good works they do. The terrible oaths and silly rituals you must submit to are justified away by thinking that all this is just ancient tradition, and surely I would never be called upon to bring harm to anyone. Let's face it folks, most people are followers, and most peoples' thoughts run on the shallow side. Granted these are broad generalities, but doesn't life's experience prove me right, to a degree?

CHAPTER XI

THERE IS A SOLUTION

Actually, you probably would not have continued into this book, unless you were inclined towards a deeper line of thought, than JOE SIX PACK. I am sure that sizable portions of the citizens of the U.S. are aware of the fact that we have many serious problems here. But it never ceases to amaze me, the amount of crap that people will put with before taking any sort of action. We endured the great depression, we see our hard earned tax dollars piddled away... given away to every nation on earth, for every "off the wall" reason under the sun. Now Clinton is going to give 100 million dollars to Israel, etc. And still we sit back and watch and vote. Yes we vote and they put another Mason in office to carry out the clandestine agenda of the ruling elite. WHY BOTHER??? It has gone on since time immemorial; sheep lead around by the nose. If you know anything about sheep, they live by herd instinct. If one breaks and runs over the cliff, the rest of the herd follows, instinctively. Jews were carried to the slaughter without a fight... people used and then buried. People in the U.S. are once again feeling the crunch. Ma and Pa both have to join the slave train and work a job just to prove some form of semi-dignified existence. Yes, I would tend to say folks are getting fed up. But the kings of the world know they can push harder, and suck more blood before all hell breaks loose. They know their sociology lessons well. What can we do? How can we form a more perfect union? Obviously there is room for much improvement. Will we take some sort of positive action to regain charge of our lives? If not for ourselves, but at least for our children? Will we be lead off like the Jews, without a fight? Will we continue to throw up our hands with the excuse that we are overpowered and must submit?

As I said in the beginning of the book, I have some sound solutions to these questions. As to their implementation, I have no control, there. But no one can deny that they are solid tactics to take control of our lives. Here is my idea of a method of forming a more perfect union. First off, let's reaffirm some basic facts. It's the squeaky wheel that gets the grease. Trite, but true. If no demands are made, then no demand will be addressed. And it is a fact, that throughout history, the ruling elite quickly forget, because of their affluent preoccupation, like where their bread and butter comes from. Where does their bread and butter come from? It comes from the blood, sweat, and tears of the masses. Without us, they have nothing. In the U.S., the status quo is also maintained by selling the American public a bill of goods that implies Americans have power and say so in their government. The outward expression of this power is the supposed right to vote. If you believe your vote matters, then you believe in the system as it exists, and you indicate to the ruling elite that you believe in their package of propaganda. It means you have a certain amount of faith in the system, as it is, and accept for better or worse. Nothing, and I repeat, NOTHING worries and angers the ruling elite more than the citizen who refuses to vote.

Let's face it, as citizens there aren't many avenues we can take to put across our message, legally that is... Refusal to vote puts across a strong message to those in power. It says, quite simply, I don't buy into your propaganda, and I am aware of the fact that my vote means nothing, and was never meant to mean anything. When you don't vote, you are still voting. This may sound weird, but by not voting, you still cast a vote... a vote of apathy. You see, the ruling elite know exactly how many eligible voters there are in this country, and they know exactly how many of these eligible voters, voted. So when the vote tally is done and, it is realized, for example, out of 100 percent of the eligible voters, only 25 percent voted, and 75 percent did not vote, this tells the establishment that 75 percent of the eligible voters cast a vote of apathy. In other words, 75 percent of the eligible votes felt it wasn't worth their time to bother to vote. They felt that no matter who got into office, the "same screw the public" business would transpire. This is why the establishment is so worried about getting people to vote. When the turnout for voting is very low it makes them look bad, and puts forth the message in strong terms that we don't have any faith in their corrupt system. This is one of the biggest slaps in the face that a citizen can give. If we intend to change things, we must get the message across and that for once we want our share of the pie.

In order to get our message across we must speak loudly to be heard, and not voting puts forth a loud message. It is quite simple, make the vote fair or I won't play! Get rid of the Electoral College, "and give me my fair share or else." In the beginning of the book I stated that in my opinion, the old method of bloody revolt to accomplish change is futile. I still adamantly defend this idea. Open revolt is fruitless and ugly. The common folks are the ones who pay the price in suffering and bloodshed. It has been tried time and again throughout the ages, and always the ruling elite takes charge and gains back the power. Anyway, for the purpose of this book and our situation here in the U.S., total overthrow is not wanted or necessary. All that is necessary is to demand our fair share, and to be heard. We should strive to let the establishment know that the old tricks aren't working and any new tricks will be dealt with firmly. We are tired of being lied to and stolen from... If these messages are put forth by the common public, the ruling elite will cough up a larger portion of the fruits of our labor. These folks who run the show do respond to and understand only one language that is power and force. If our numbers speak loud enough, they will respond in kind. But if the working public refuses to speak loudly or remains defeated without a fight, the elite will simply continue to bleed the small guy to death.

I am sure the establishment would have a field day with me and this book, probably would hang me if they could. But, let me remind you that I am not advocating anarchy or bloody revolt. My only message is that for once in our history we the people insist that the establishment be accountable to us and serves our needs. I am not advocating throwing the baby out with the bath water. I am sure some will read this book and of course label me a traitor, etc., but the fact of the matter is that I have a great stake in the betterment of this country, and a love for it. My roots in this country go deep, maybe even deeper than most because of my Native American heritage, and maybe because of my inherent need for justice. Who are the real traitors here, me or the businessman who moves his company to Mexico, Brazil, or Taiwan? Would I be labeled any more a traitor than presidents who give 10 billion dollars to Russia? (I understand the Russians have lately acquired a taste for Marlboro cigarettes.)

Would I be any more a traitor than Clinton who gave 40 billion dollars to Mexico and 100 million to Israel? I ask again, who are the traitors here? Call me what you like, but I call them as I see them. I will readily admit that I am tired of getting shafted, watching it happen and knowing who is doing it. Unlike the Jews, American Indians fight back! So I've put forth the facts that I have discovered over the years, into this book. I've outlined a definite problem, and at this point offered some solutions, number one being, the vote or lack thereof. The vote of apathy, the Achilles heel of the right side... Bang. And now I will concentrate on the Achilles heel of the left side. This is the second show of power, and the only way I know of to drive our message home, MONEY... Without our tax dollars to fund their greed and unaccountability, the establishment has nothing. They must be reminded of where their money comes from. Many people have approached the issue by suggesting we refuse to pay our taxes. They think that will make a strong personal statement that, "We are fed up with the establishment's irresponsibility." Sorry folks, it won't work, you're beat from the start. It's illegal and a one-man army never accomplished anything. Of course, it is not illegal to refuse to go to work. There is no law against calling in sick. A nationwide work stoppage would put forth a strong message, and of course, no tax revenue would be generated.

This is the Achilles heel of the left side. Would it work? You bet it would! Your message would be conveyed swiftly and in no uncertain terms. I need not say any more about this tactic. It is powerful and it speaks for itself. Let me make myself clear about this, I don't claim to have all the answers, but I do have two of the hardest hitting legal tactics that I know of to offer as a solution to our serious problem. I emphasize the word LEGAL. Neither of my two solutions is illegal. In summary, we have two tools with which to combat the evil, which are perfectly legal and effective. Number one, the vote of apathy, putting forth the message that we are hip to your game and we are no longer playing. Number two, a national moratorium on work for two or three days. So, as I promised in the beginning of the book, I offer two solid solutions to our problem, which I truly believe would have a profound effect in conveying a message. I readily admit that at this point, I cannot go any further. I am not an organizer and would not know where to begin. Maybe someone out there will read this and know where to start. The only part I am able to play in forming a more perfect union is to put my discoveries on paper and offer some sound solutions. The rest is up to you.

PLATE 1

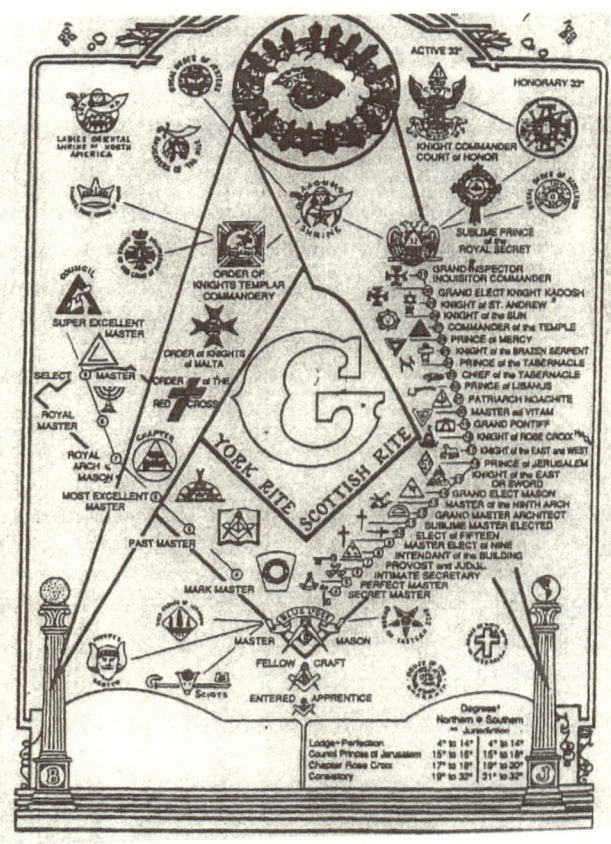

Note the all seeing eye. The all seeing eyes appear on the back of our one dollar bill atop the pyramid. It is an important Masonic symbol.

PLATE 2

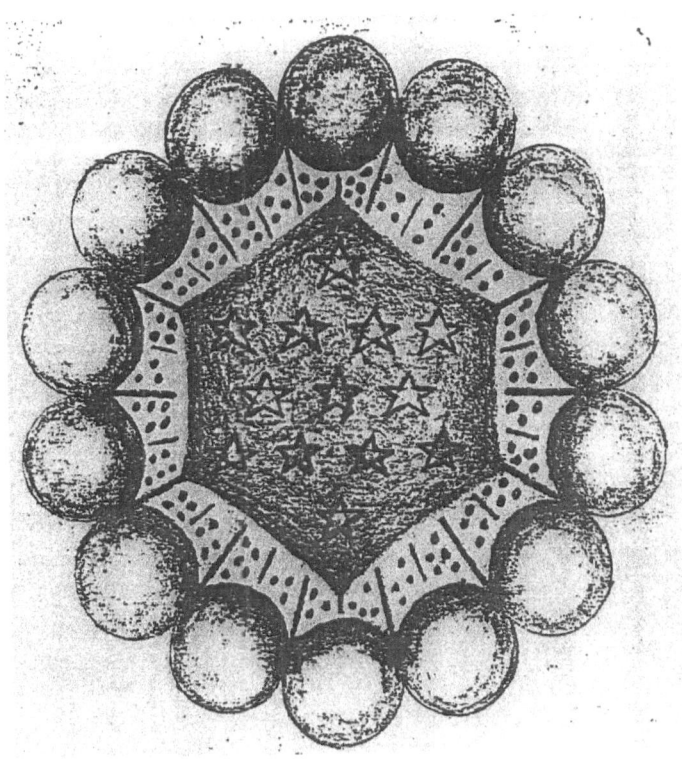

This is the same symbol above the eagle on the back of the one dollar bill with the star of David plainly outlined by me to illustrate the now plainly visible star of David on the back of our one dollar bill.

PLATE 3

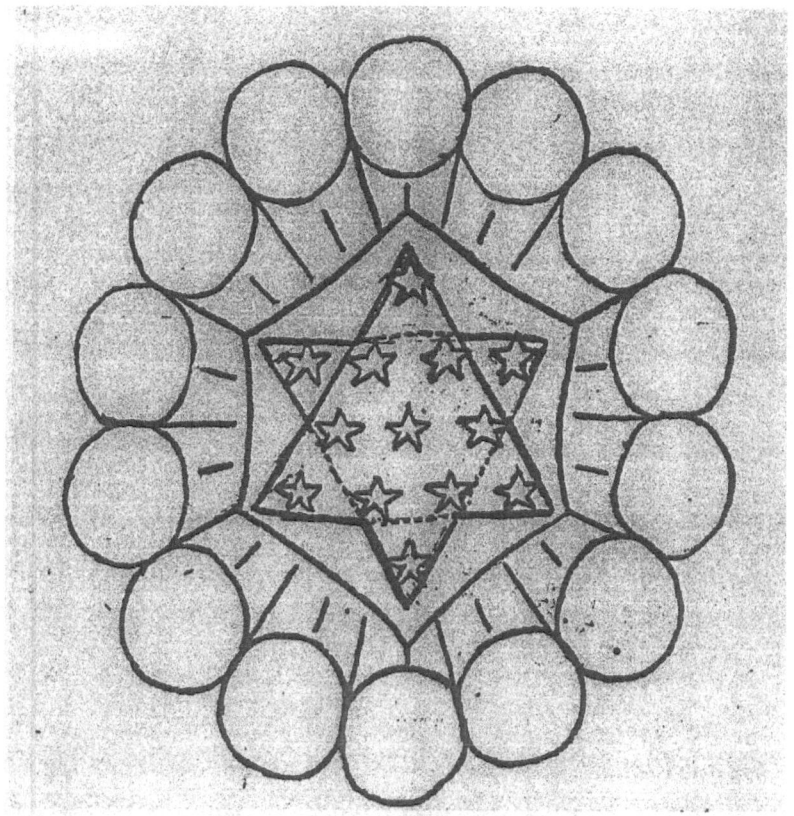

This is the same symbol above the eagle on the back of the one dollar bill with the star of David plainly outlined by me to illustrate the now plainly visible star of David on the back of our one dollar bill.

PLATE 4

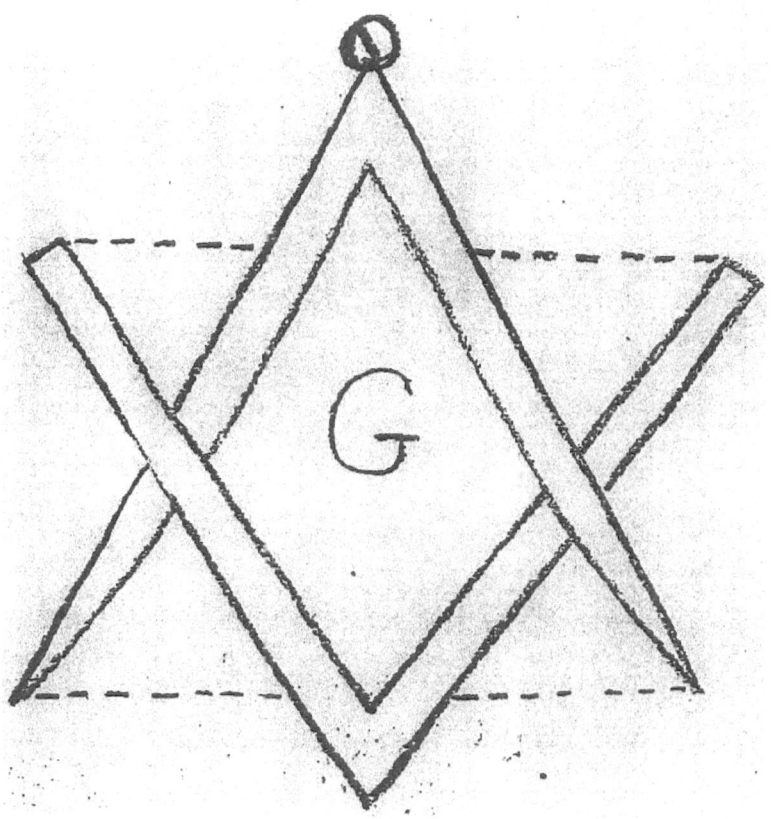

Surely it is no coincidence that the greatest and most revered symbol of the Free Masonry, the compass, square, and G forms a star of David if you simply connect the dotted lines. That same star of David on the one dollar bill represents free Masonary and it's connection with the Jewish Kabula.

PLATE 5

Of course free masonry would argue that their famous compass and square is not illustrated in a manor which would resemble the star of David. They would argue that it is and always has been illustrated as pictured in plate 6, see plate 6. I contend that it is illustrated in many styles. Some of the styles can easily be fashioned into the star of David, such as the above style Draw your dotted line and you have the star of David. Incidentally the above compass and square comes directly from the book called Encyclopedia of free Masonry, a famous Masonic book, totally accepted by Free Masons.

PLATE 6

PLATE 7

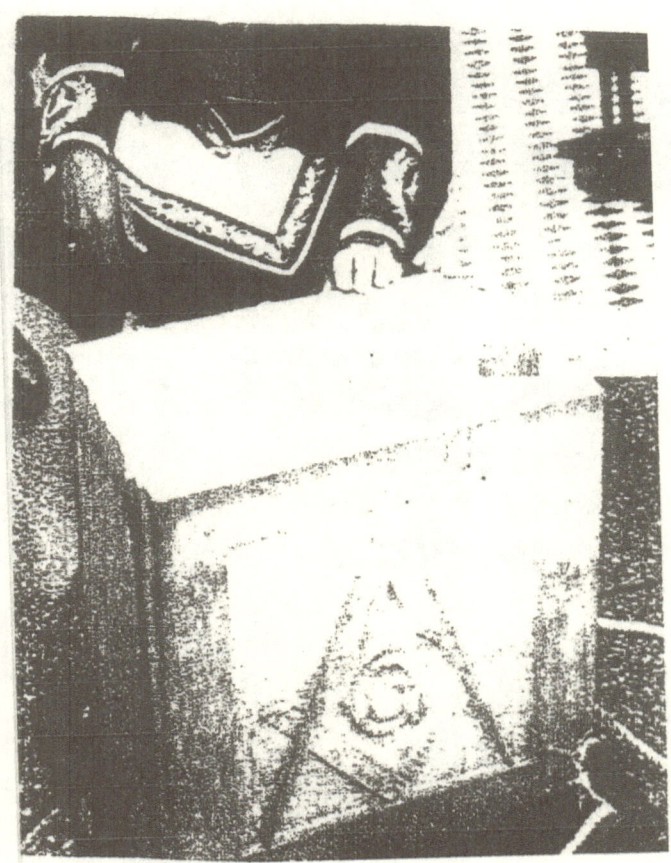

This an accurate copy of the corner stone of the capital building layed by George Washington.

PLATE 8

George Washington Laying the Cornerstone of the United States Capitol, Sept. 18, 1793

This is an oil painting of old George laying the Masonic corner stone of the capital building, note his masonic apron and other masonic do dads

PLATE 9

This is flag of the president of the United States. Note the four fallen stars by the eagles head symbolizing the colonies not needed to ratify the constitution. All pictorial symbolism, Masonic or goverment is well thought out and nothing is left to coincidence.

PLATE 10
More examples of Masonic Hokos Pokos

PLATE 11
More examples of Masonic Hokos Pokos

FIRST & LAST STONE OF THE JERUSALEM CHURCH.

We Have Found It

FREE MASON'S AT WORK.

PLATE 12
More examples of Masonic Hokos Pokos

OLD AND NEW IERUSALEM BUILDING.

FREE MASONRY CROWN'D
DEDICATED TO THE LEARNED BROTHERS.